Praise for *Learn Like a Leader*

"Some of our greatest contemporary leaders have shared their leadership wisdom and experience in *Learn Like a Leader*. Each story shares a lesson we make our own. And the best leadership lessons come from leaders themselves who have the courage to tell others about difficult situations they faced, how they handled them, and what happened as a result. Read and reread each story and you will discover what it is to *Learn Like a Leader*!"

—Frances Hesselbein, president and CEO, Leader to Leader Institute and former CEO, Girl Scouts of the USA

"One of the things that sets the best leaders apart is the ability to communicate complex ideas in a simple way. Stories have always been the best way to do this, as they provide guidance about desired choices in a persuasive and memorable manner. This book is full of powerful stories by leaders who teach leaders."

— Norm Smallwood, coauthor, *The Leadership Code* and *Leadership Brand*

"If good leaders are good storytellers—and they are—then pull up your favorite chair to hear the voices of these top leadership experts. The tales of turning points in their lives—so vividly told here—will inspire, entertain, and instruct us all."

—John Alexander, executive coach and former president, Center for Creative Leadership

"A remarkable collection of inspiration, wisdom, and insight from the true luminaries in our field. The lessons shared in this book are not to be missed!"

—Marc Effron, president, The Talent Strategy Group

"The greatest leaders in history have understood the power of stories for developing themselves and others. And this book distills decades of leadership wisdom through insightful and inspiring stories. Every leader should have this book."

—Mark Murphy, chairman and CEO, Leadership IQ

"It's tempting to approach leadership as a unified discipline with well-known rules and approaches that somehow lead to high leadership effectiveness as long as all the rules are followed faithfully. But leadership is just not like that. In practice it's usually messy, inscrutable, and resistant to simple classification. *Learn Like a Leader* reflects this reality with a kaleidoscopic view that includes the deep life experience of leaders. I empathize with the honesty of an approach that pays homage to the richness and complexity of leadership and leaders. I think that readers looking for acknowledgement of this fact will really get a lot out of this book."

—Dr. E. Ted Prince, founder and CEO, Perth Leadership Institute

"This book is a delicious read. The autobiographical voice encourages us to identify with the writer-speaker and recall our own experiences that created the same kind of awareness the authors describe. Each contributor is an authority whose wisdom we have long enjoyed, but in describing their personal experiences we also come to like that person. This is a marvelous book to dip into and savor, returning to it over and over again."

—Judith M. Bardwick, PhD, volunteer clinical professor of psychiatry, UCSD and author of *One Foot Out the Door and Danger in the Comfort Zone*

"*Learn Like a Leader: Top Leaders Share Their Learning Journeys* is a superb collection of writings on why leadership matters. In it, Ken Shelton, Marshall Goldsmith, and Bev Kaye have gathered together a remarkable group of thought leaders who share their deep insights into how to be an effective and caring leader. An important book for those who desire better leadership."

—Larry C. Spears, president and CEO, The Spears Center for Servant-Leadership

"For years, I have worked to inspire people to identify, realize, and sustain their One Dream. As the many contributors to this book witness, great leaders are eager learners and able teachers and coaches who inspire team members to join them on the journey to realize their shared dream."

—Lance Secretan, author of *The Spark, the Flame and the Torch*

LEARN LIKE A LEADER

Today's Top Leaders Share Their Learning Journeys

EDITORS

MARSHALL GOLDSMITH

BEVERLY KAYE

KEN SHELTON

NICHOLAS BREALEY
PUBLISHING

BOSTON · LONDON

First published by Nicholas Brealey Publishing in 2010.

20 Park Plaza, Suite 1115A
Boston, MA 02116, USA
Tel: + 617-523-3801
Fax: + 617-523-3708

3-5 Spafield Street, Clerkenwell
London, EC1R 4QB, UK
Tel: +44-(0)-207-239-0360
Fax: +44-(0)-207-239-0370

www.nicholasbrealey.com

Printed in the United States of America

14 13 12 11 10   1 2 3 4 5

ISBN: 978-1-85788-557-6

Library of Congress Cataloging-in-Publication Data
   Learn like a leader : today's top leaders share their learning journeys /
editors, Marshall Goldsmith, Beverly Kaye, Ken Shelton.
      p. cm.
   Rev. ed. of: Learning journeys. c2000.
   This book is one product of a Learning Network weekend conference.
   ISBN 978-1-85788-557-6
   1. Executives—Training of—Congresses.   2. Leadership—Study and
teaching—Congresses.   3. Mentoring in business—Congresses.   4. Storytelling—
Congresses.   I. Goldsmith, Marshall.   II. Kaye, Beverly L.   III. Shelton, Ken,
1947--IV. Learning journeys.
   HD30.4.L396 2010
   658.4'07124—dc22

                                                                2010013526

Contents

UNLEARNING WHAT YOU THOUGHT WAS SO

PAIN IS A GREAT TEACHER

Preface

More than a decade ago, The Learning Network (TLN), a group of senior thought leaders in the field of management and organization development, met in beautiful Del Mar, California. The meeting took place over a weekend in January, not long after the New Year, carrying with it the same expectations and wishes that resolutions often do.

The TLN weekend, then and now, is devoted to learning how our work interconnects, thinking about the future, and designing projects that enable us to "give back" to the world. Numerous ideas have been generated at these retreats, and while many have never made it off the brainstorming table, several have lasted and made a positive difference. This book is one of them.

During one brainstorming session, we decided to focus on how we, as experienced leaders, learn. This was in striking contrast to our usual work—helping others learn! Yet we found that we could not only learn from each other, but from a great many of the thought leaders in our field. The idea of learning how great teachers learn fascinated us. It was in this spirit that *Learn Like a Leader* was born.

When we asked one hundred of the most prominent figures in the field of management and organization development to describe a personal learning experience—a turning point that shaped their life's work and influenced their teachings—we got some amazing stories, thirty-five of which are shared here. As you read these stories, you'll see the subjects come to life as coaches and mentors, and we bet you'll identify with both their genius and their humanness. These management thinkers see learning as a process; they retell their personal stories to offer fresh insights, uncover new challenges, and lead others to contribute more of their full potential. They teach the value of self-knowledge and reflection, motivating us to discover and describe our own "learning journeys"—to find our own voices, uncover our own answers, and share our stories with others.

Everyone's life is filled with experiences, whether they are traumatic, rewarding, frustrating, or humiliating. All of these can be sources of valuable learning. Some people are more adept at reflecting on the meaning of these experiences than others, but all of us understand the power of storytelling. We enjoy reading about other people: their stories tap our emotions and intellects, helping us remember and learn.

This book suggests that all of us can learn to examine our lives, reflect on our successes and failures, and tune in to the music of our own stories. We can look to experiences in our lives for wisdom and guidance.

And so what started so many years ago as a collection of stories about the people in that room became a much larger collection of stories by leaders and thinkers who made significant contributions to the field of management development. Lists were drawn; networks were shared; calls were made. The work began, and what seemed like an easy job in the beginning became, well, a journey in and of itself!

The world has changed a lot since the first time we met as a group. And we've realized that, as organizations must incorporate sustainability, efficiency, branding, and morale-building into a system that is also profitable, the learning industry is more important now than it has ever been. Out of that realization came a decision: to donate royalties from this book to the Peter Drucker Foundation for Nonprofit Management. This foundation does exceptional work in providing leadership resources and development opportunities. It also provides a forum for thought leaders in our field to share their latest ideas. This was our way of "giving back" to the leadership community.

As we go to press on *Learn Like a Leader*, we also wish to pay tribute to one of the founding members of The Learning Network, Dick Beckhard—a true leader in our field and, more importantly, a wonderful human being. He greatly supported us in this and many of our other efforts. We feel it is appropriate to dedicate this book to Dick.

As we read the stories in this collection, many of which have stood the test of time, we still find many things we can directly relate to, or at least empathize with. More than abstract concepts, these stories make for enjoyable, memorable reading that leads to greater insight. We hope these learning journeys, along with the personal reflection questions asked by each storyteller in this book, will help unearth greater meaning for people in families, groups, businesses, governments, and other communities. We hope that *Learn Like a Leader* will help you to learn from the stories that unfold in your own life, too!

A PERSONAL NOTE

Beverly Kaye has truly been the "heart and soul" of this *Learn Like a Leader* project. She originated the idea, developed the concept, and helped us all "hang in there" until the project was successfully completed. Without her ongoing drive, support, and inspiration, this book would have never happened.

One of my great learning journeys has been the opportunity to work with Bev on this project. She has an amazing spirit that is contagious. She never lets day-to-day hassles get her down or remove her joy in her profession and her life. She has the gift of making every day seem like a wonderful learning journey!

Speaking for everyone who has contributed to making this book a reality, I would like to say "Thank you!" to Beverly Kaye.

Marshall Goldsmith

January 2010

Acknowledgments

The main acknowledgment for this work goes, without question, to the storytellers who took the time and the energy to share a development moment with our readers. Those who appeared in our first edition were asked to review their stories and change them if they wished. Some did because they felt they had a better story to tell; others felt the original story remained an important turning point. New storytellers joined us and enriched the process and the result. We appreciate their candidness, and the thought that went into deciding what to share and what provocative questions to ask their readers.

Appreciation goes to Jodi Knox, who worked with us on the first edition and made an important contribution to the second edition as well. Her deep interest in leadership, coaching, and personal growth drew her to developing this compendium of stories both times. You will see her recommendations for action strategies at the end of this book. She now leads a leadership development and executive coaching practice as the founder of Action Dialogue Associates. Milo Sindell, cofounder of Hit the Ground Running, a firm that provides software solutions for employee performance, was on our team for both editions as well. His ideas and suggestions were put to use as we revised, rethought, and repositioned this information.

A huge thank you goes to Sarah McArthur, editor and assistant to Marshall Goldsmith. Sarah put her time and attention on reconnecting with all our contributors and reaching out with several new invitations. Without Sarah's organizational talents and awesome attention to detail, this whole project would still be in first gear! Sarah's upbeat, "can-do" attitude kept us moving from start to finish.

My colleague and friend Marshall Goldsmith used his "life is good" mantra, his network of friends, and some good positive cheerleading to make this feel doable in the midst of all that each of us had already on our plates! Ken Shelton, editor of *Leadership Excellence* and *Personal Excellence,* gave his continued support.

I came up with the idea, but had no conception of the time and attention this would require in either the first or second edition. Luckily, I had great colleagues as sounding boards. As a career practitioner for several decades, I have always believed in the power of story and its use in gaining new ideas for varied development directions. The stories here will speak to those who need to ponder and learn from these individual messages about leadership, choice, and chance.

My own research in employee engagement tells me that all of us crave authentic conversations with our peers and leaders. The stories here were selected because they provide food for thought. They are critical for mentoring, coaching, and professional growth. I have been taught by all who were associated with this project. We hope it teaches you.

Beverly Kaye

Introduction

Learning from Experience

The most powerful learning is that which occurs through experience. While we cannot experience all that is to be learned firsthand, we can learn through the experiences of others. You probably already have individuals in your life that have played a part in your learning. The benefit of *Learn Like a Leader* is that you have the opportunity to learn from some prominent figures in the field of leadership development from the last fifty years.

Learn Like a Leader is divided into eight themes that range from learning from difficult or painful situations to understanding how you are perceived through others. All stories present the experience of the authors, what they learned from their experience, and how they have integrated that learning into their lives. Whether it is Charles Garfield's example of how we create our own reality or Jay Galbraith's story of living with and managing complexity, each story is an intimate look at the experiences and wisdom gained from them, which is passed on here for others to learn. Each author has added provocative questions at the end of each chapter, which give you the opportunity to learn from these firsthand experiences and see how you might apply their experiences to your life.

This is a book for individuals, managers, leaders, coaches, and consultants looking to develop their own leadership strengths as well as those of others. The stories told here by management thought leaders contain powerful lessons. Many of the lessons were learned outside the classroom and outside of work, for leadership lessons are wherever we find them. As the stories demonstrate, truly effective people learn from all of life, and apply their lessons to keep growing. You will find these stories about the experience of learning and growth of a very personal nature.

The power of storytelling cannot be denied. During the past decade, business leaders, trainers, and consultants have discovered it as an indispensable management and leadership tool. Numerous articles in business publications such as *Fortune*, *FastCompany*, the *Wall Street Journal*, and the *Harvard Business Review* explore the many applications of storytelling to issues such as strategic planning, leader development, corporate communications, sales, learning, and knowledge management.

In this lifelong endeavor of personal and professional development, stories are an enjoyable way to learn from others. They create an affiliation between the person who has the experience and the learner who finds him- or herself in a similar circumstance. This is especially so when the stories are told, as they are here, in very personal ways.

Many of the stories in this book will resonate on a personal level for particular individuals, and some stories can serve as general lessons for us all.

This book is divided into sections. Each story is introduced briefly and is accompanied by a set of questions that facilitate deeper exploration into the lessons and learning presented. These questions can be applied in a group setting for team building, as a continuation of your own exploration, or perhaps as a dialogue starter for your own group of friends. Use them for inspiration, as a resource, as a starting point, or as a springboard for your own ideas and creativity. We hope they help you in your own learning journey and we encourage you to use stories to share knowledge, to develop mutual understanding, and to build deeper appreciation for differences.

The afterword and epilogue provide further insight into the power of stories to help you apply these learnings as a consultant, manager, or teacher within your organization. Use them to spark a workplace forum for the exploration of individual differences, thus building the capacity of the learning organization.

Finally, the editors hope you will use these stories to create the kind of dialogue and discussion that usually does not take place in organizations. We have collected these essays and shared them with you because we passionately believe in the power of personal experience as captured in the form of story. Our stories are meant to share knowledge and wisdom, and most important, to inspire you to explore and bring to life your own experiences.

LESSONS ON LEADERSHIP

WARREN BENNIS
Write Your Own Life

JIM COLLINS
The Learning Executive

SALLY HELGESEN
A Journey to Authentic Leadership

ALAN M. WEBBER
Speaking Truth Is Power

1

WARREN BENNIS

Warren Bennis is distinguished professor of business administration and founding chairman of the Leadership Institute at the University of Southern California. He has been observing and writing about leaders and managers for more than five decades. His many books include the bestselling Leaders *and* On Becoming a Leader, *and the Pulitzer Prize–nominated* An Invented Life, *as well as* Organizing Genius, Managing People Is Like Herding Cats, *and* Old Dogs, New Tricks. *Bennis has served on the faculties of Massachusetts Institute of Technology's Sloan School of Management, Harvard University, and Boston University, and he has been executive vice president of the State University of New York at Buffalo and president of the University of Cincinnati.*

Write Your Own Life

We all face the great challenge to discover our native abilities and to invent and reinvent ourselves throughout life. I believe in self-invention as an exercise of the imagination. It is how we get to know ourselves. People who can't invent and reinvent themselves must be content with borrowed postures, secondhand ideas, and fitting in instead of standing out. Inventing oneself is the opposite of accepting the roles we were brought up to play.

To be authentic is literally to be your own author (the words derive from the same Greek root): to discover your native energies and desires, and then to find your own way of acting on them. When you do that, you are not existing simply to live up to an image posited by the culture, family tradition, or some other authority. When you write your own life, you are playing the game that is natural for you to play. You are keeping covenant with your own promise.

MY OWN ROOTS

The landscape of my childhood was very like a Beckett stage set: barren, meager, endless. A little boy waited there for someone who might not, probably would not, show up. There were walk-ons occasionally: twin brothers, ten years my senior; a father who worked eighteen hours a day (when he took off his shoes and soiled socks, the ring of dirt around his ankles had to be scrubbed off with a stiff-bristled brush); and a mother who liked vaudeville and played mah-jongg with her friends when she wasn't helping my father eke out an existence.

I was withdrawn, sullen, detached, removed from hope or desire, and probably depressed—"mopey," my father called it. I was also left pretty much alone. I had no close friends. I can't remember how I spent my time, except I know that I made up improved versions of my life that ran like twenty-four-hour newsreels in my mind.

I didn't much like school, and I barely remember my teachers, except for Miss Shirer. I liked Miss Shirer enormously. She taught the eighth grade, and she was almost famous because her older brother, William Shirer, was broadcasting from Berlin on CBS. I leaned into the radio whenever Shirer was on. That he was anti-Hitler was thrilling to a kid who, in 1938, often felt like the only Jew in Westwood, New Jersey, a town that richly deserved its reputation as a major stronghold of the German Bund.

On one momentous occasion, Miss Shirer asked us to spend about ten minutes telling the class about our favorite hobby. I panicked. After all, I liked Miss Shirer a lot, but the truth was that I didn't have anything remotely like a favorite hobby. My efforts to develop recreational interests like those of the other guys had failed miserably. I was mediocre at sports. I was bored with collecting stamps. I was too clumsy to tie dry flies, too nervous to hunt, and too maladroit to build model airplanes out of balsa wood. What I finally decided to do, in a moment of desperate inspiration, was to bring in a box full of shoe polish, different colors and shades in cans and bottles, since the only palpable physical activity I regularly engaged in was shining the family shoes.

And so, when it was my turn in the spotlight, I revealed the arcane nature of a new art form. I described in loving detail the nuances of my palette (I was especially good on the subtle differences between oxblood and maroon). I discoursed on the form and function of the various appliances needed to achieve an impressive tone and sheen. I argued both sides of the debate on solid versus liquid wax and wrapped it all up with a spirited disquisition on the multiple virtues of neat's-foot oil. It was a remarkable performance, if only because it was, from start to finish, an act of pure imagination. I could tell from her smile that Miss Shirer thought it was terrific. Even the class seemed impressed in a stupefied way. And there, in a flourish of brushes and shoe polish, a new Warren Bennis was born.

ARMY AND SCHOOL

When I graduated from high school into the army during World War II (1943–1947), I saw firsthand the consequences of good and bad leadership in the simplest and starkest terms—morale, tank support that would or would not be where it was supposed to be, wounds, and body counts. The army was the first organization I was to observe close-up and in depth. And although I have been in more pleasant classrooms, it was an excellent place to study such organizational realities as the effects of command-and-control leadership and the paralyzing impact of institutional bureaucracy. The army also taught me the value of being organized.

Once out of the army, I attended Antioch College (1947–1951), where I learned to have opinions. That may not sound very important, but it amounted to a personal paradigm shift. What freedom, what liberation it was to have opinions. Having opinions was, at least for me, tantamount to developing a personal identity.

To get through the Ph.D. program at MIT (1951–1956), I began to memorize and mimic. I imitated my professors and the brightest of my fellow graduate students. For roughly two years, I lip-synched what I heard. Eventually, the words I formed on my lips came more naturally, but I often wondered whether I was kidding myself.

From 1955 to 1971, I made stops in Bethel, Maine, where everyone was buzzing over Kurt Lewin's T-groups; Boston University, where I taught psychology and underwent psychoanalysis; and SUNY Buffalo, where I learned that unless a vision is sustained by action, it quickly turns to ashes.

UNIVERSITY PRESIDENT

As president of the University of Cincinnati (1971 to 1978), I finally realized that my principal role model would have to be me. I decided that the kind of university president I wanted to be was one who led, not managed. That's an important difference. Many an institution is well managed yet poorly led. The staff may excel in the ability to handle all the daily routines, yet they never ask whether the routine should be engaged in the first place.

My entrapment in minutiae made me realize another thing: People were following the old army game. They did not want to take responsibility for the decisions they needed to make. "Let's push up the tough ones" had become the motto. As a result, everybody was dumping his or her "wet babies" (as old hands at the State Department called them) on my desk. I decided then and there that my highest priority was to create an "executive constellation" to run the office of the president. The sole requirements for inclusion in the group were that the individual needed to know more than I did about his or her area of competence and had to be willing to take care of daily matters without referring them back to me. I was going to make the time to lead.

I realized that I had been doing what so many leaders do. I was trying to be everything to the organization: father, fixer, policeman, ombudsman, rabbi, therapist, and banker. As a CEO who was similarly afflicted put it to me later, "If I'm walking on the shop floor and see a leak in the dike, I have to stick my finger in." Trying to be everything to everyone was diverting me from real leadership. It was burning me out. And perhaps worst of all, it was denying all the potential leaders under me the chance to learn and prove themselves.

Things got better after that, although I never came close to the ideal. As I look back at my experience at UC, I compare it with my psychoanalysis: I wouldn't have missed it for the world, and I would never go through it again. In becoming a leader I learned a number of important things about both leadership and myself. As Sophocles observes in *Antigone*, "But hard it is to learn the mind of any mortal, or the heart, 'til he be tried in chief authority. Power shows the man."

Having executive power showed me some personal truths. First, I was, as the song says, "Looking for love in all the wrong places." Intellectually, I knew that leaders can't, and shouldn't, count on being loved. But I seriously underestimated the emotional impact of angry constituents. I believed the false dream that people would love me if only they really got to know me.

Anyone in authority is to some extent the hostage of how others perceive him or her. The perceptions of other people can be a prison. For the first time I began to understand what it must be like to be the victim of prejudice, to be helpless in the steel embrace of how other people see you. People impute motives to their leaders, love or hate them, seek them out or avoid them, and idolize or demonize them, independent of what the leaders do or who they are. Ironically, at the very time I had the most power, I felt the greatest sense of powerlessness.

And I realized an important personal truth. I was never going to be completely happy with positional power, the only kind of power an organization can bestow. What I really wanted was personal power, influence based on voice.

THE AUTUMN OF MY DAYS

USC has been my longest continuous tenure at any institution. In many ways it has been the happiest period of my life. USC has provided me with exactly the right social architecture to do what seems most important to me now: teaching in the broadest sense.

At USC I have the leisure to consolidate what I've learned about self-invention, about the importance of organization, about the nature of change, and about the nature of leadership, as well as to find ways to communicate those lessons. Erik Erikson talks about an eight-stage process of human development. I think I have entered Erikson's seventh stage, the generative one, in which self-absorption gives way to an altruistic surrender to the next generation. Although writing is my greatest joy, I also take enormous pleasure in people-growing, in watching others bloom, in mentoring as I was mentored.

What I have discovered is that the need to reinvent oneself, to "compose a life," as Mary Catherine Bateson puts it, is ongoing. A few years before he died, my closest friend, Sam Jaffe (who in his fifties was the Academy Award–winning producer of *Born Free*) and I took a summer course on Dickens at Trinity Hall, Cambridge. Sam, who tried to buy the film rights to a book I had given him, continued in his nineties to scrimmage in the notoriously competitive subculture of Hollywood. He gave me hope.

I find that I have acquired a new set of priorities. Some of the old agonies have simply disappeared. I have no doubt that my three children are more important than anything else in my life. Having achieved a certain level of worldly success, I need hardly think about it anymore. Gentler virtues seem terribly important now. I strive to be generous and productive. I would hope to be thought of as a decent and creative man.

I think Miss Shirer would be proud.

QUESTIONS

‡ *What do you think are your native abilities?*

‡ *How are you currently using those abilities, and how would you like to use them in the future?*

‡ *Are you living a life that would make a former teacher, parent, or coach proud of you?*

2   JIM COLLINS

Jim Collins is a student and teacher of enduring great companies—how they grow, how they attain superior performance, and how good companies can become great companies. Jim has authored or coauthored four books, including Built to Last, Good to Great, *and* How the Mighty Fall. *His work has been featured in* Fortune, The Wall Street Journal, BusinessWeek, Harvard Business Review, *and* Fast Company. *For a comprehensive list of the books and articles he has published, go to* www.jimcollins.com.

The Learning Executive

How would your day be different if you organized your time, energy, and resources primarily around the objective of learning, instead of around performance? For many people, their daily activities—what they do and how they go about doing it—would be dramatically changed. Indeed, despite all the buzz around the concept of the "learning organization," I'm struck by how few people seem to have embraced the idea of being a true learning person.

This came home to me during an interview with a television producer developing a documentary on Sam Walton. After about forty-five minutes, she asked if I had anything else to add, indicating the end of the interview. "No," I said, "but I'd like to ask you some questions." She paused, obviously not prepared for my request, and then gave an uncertain, "Okay." For the next fifteen minutes, I had the great pleasure of asking her questions about what she had learned in her research. The producer had no background in business—having done most of her documentaries on historical figures like Stalin and Mozart—so I thought she might have a fresh and illuminating perspective. She did, and I learned some new information and gained new insights about one of my favorite subjects.

"That's the first time that's ever happened to me," she said. "I interview professors and experts all the time, but I've never had one turn the tables and begin asking me questions. At first I was taken aback—surprised really—but it's refreshing to see that experts can still learn."

Stop and think about that for a minute. Here's a bright television producer who spends her life delving into specific subjects—a walking treasure trove of knowledge—and people whose profession is to continually learn don't pause to take the opportunity to expand their expertise further by talking with her. They act as knowers rather than learners, which, incidentally, is just the opposite of what Sam Walton did.

Walton viewed himself not as a definitive expert on retailing but as a lifelong student of his craft, always asking questions and taking every opportunity to learn. A Brazilian businessman once told me that of ten U.S. retailing CEOs he wrote to asking for an appointment after he'd purchased a discount retailing chain in South America, only Walton said yes. "We didn't know much about retailing, so we wanted to talk to executives who knew the business," he explained. "Most didn't bother to reply. Sam said, 'Sure, come on up.' Only later did I realize he was as interested in learning from us as we were in learning from him; he pummeled us with questions about Brazil. Later, we launched a joint venture with Wal-Mart in South America."

Becoming a learning person certainly involves responding to every situation with learning in mind, as Walton did. But it involves more than that; it requires setting explicit learning objectives. Look at your personal list of long-term objectives, your midterm objectives, and your current to-do list. How many items fall into the performance genre and how many fall into the learning genre? How many begin with the structure "My objective is to learn X," rather than "My objective is to accomplish Y"? Most people operate off of to-do lists. They're a useful mechanism for getting things done. A true learning person also has a "to-learn" list, and the items on that list carry at least as much weight in how one organizes his or her time as the to-do list.

Granite Rock, in Watsonville, California, one of the few authentic learning organizations, has institutionalized this idea by replacing performance goals for individuals with learning goals. The stone, concrete, and asphalt supplier makes the shift explicit by asking each employee to set his or her annual objectives in the format "Learn _____ so that I can _____."

Learning people also develop explicit learning mechanisms, such as "learning logs" or formal "autopsies"—time explicitly set aside to discuss or reflect on events and extract the maximum knowledge and understanding from them. Such people plant seeds of learning that will flower later. One prominent thinker I spent a day with ended our discussion with the statement, "I have a small consulting fee: you must keep me informed as to your learning and progress." Every six months or so I send him a letter, and I imagine he gets dozens of such learning letters a year. I've also found the mechanism of a learning notebook to be useful; in it I keep track of my learning and observations about life, work, myself, or whatever seems interesting, much the same way a scientist keeps a lab book on any subject of inquiry. It's a powerful mechanism for identifying not only learning but also the activities where I'm not learning (which I then unplug or redesign).

I'm not yet as much of a learning person as I'd like to be. Like most Americans, I'm driven largely by an urge to perform, accomplish, achieve, and get things done. Yet as I begin to consciously shift to filtering everything through a learning lens, I find both dramatic and subtle differences in the way I do things and how I spend my time. With a "get things done" lens, I'll leave a voice-mail; with a learning lens, I'll seek a real-time phone call during which I can ask questions and learn from conversation. With a performance lens, I'll try to impress the interviewer with my knowledge; with a learning lens, I'll ask her questions. Even mundane activities like washing dishes, shaving, and walking through airports can be transformed by carrying a portable tape player and listening to unabridged books on tape.

John W. Gardner, author of the classic book *Self-Renewal: The Individual and Innovative Society* (and a man who kept an active learning and teaching schedule well into his 80s), captured the spirit of the learning person with his admonition "Don't set out in life to be an interesting person; set out to be an interested person." Learning people, of which Gardner is a prime example, learn till the day they die, not because learning will "get them somewhere," but because they see learning as part of the reason for living. When asked for an economic justification for learning, they find the question as odd as being asked for a financial justification for breathing. The link between learning and performance is self-evident, but for a true learning person (or organization, for that matter), performance is not the ultimate why of learning. Learning is the why of learning. And until we grasp that fact and organize accordingly, we will not—indeed cannot—build the elusive learning organization.

QUESTIONS

✣   *How would your life be different if you organized your time, energy, and resources around the objective of learning, rather than around performance?*

✣   *If you look at your personal list of long-term, midterm, and short-term objectives, how many items fall into the performance genre and how many into the learning genre?*

✣   *Does your "to-learn" list carry at least as much weight as your to-do list?*

3   SALLY HELGESEN

Sally Helgesen is a bestselling author, speaker, and leadership consultant. Her five books include The Female Advantage: Women's Ways of Leadership, *a classic work in print for twenty years, and* The Web of Inclusion: A New Architecture for Building Great Organizations, *cited in* The Wall Street Journal *as one of the best books on leadership of all time. Sally has delivered keynotes and seminars at hundreds of the world's top institutions. Clients include Microsoft; IBM; Johnson & Johnson; Ernst & Young; Textron; The US Army College of War; The World Bank; AARP; The Council of Independent Colleges; The Office of Public Management UK; The Center for Distributed Education, Oslo; and ING Paris. She has taught at the Harvard School of Education and consulted with The United Nations Development Program on building more inclusive programs in Africa and Asia. Her new book,* The Female Vision: Women's Real Power at Work, *coauthored with Julie Johnson, will be published in May 2010.*

A Journey to Authentic Leadership

 In 1990, I published *The Female Advantage: Women's Ways of Leadership*. It was the first book to focus on what women had to contribute to organizations rather than how they needed to change and adapt. The topic generated a lot of attention and the book found an audience that has kept it in print for more than twenty years.

This success positioned me as an expert speaker on women's leadership, and I soon found myself viewed as a voice for—even a leader among—women. For the first few years, I felt awkward in this role. My academic background was unrelated to the book's topic, my own career trajectory had been unorthodox, and my cultural background taught humility as a virtue. Who was I to speak on behalf of women who had accomplished so much?

My discomfort was sharpened by the title of the book, which could be interpreted to suggest that I reflected or even embodied the advantage of which I wrote. I was also unsure how my new role jibed with my view of myself as "just a writer," an objective observer who reported on what she saw rather than sharing the experience of her subjects. I made sure to start each talk by noting the fortuitous, even accidental, nature of my expertise.

One morning when presenting to a group of female engineers in Silicon Valley, I was asked to describe one thing participants could do the following day to gain greater visibility in their organizations. The answers came easily because I had spent a lot of time interviewing women who had seen their work undervalued. I talked about how women needed to claim their achievements rather than expecting others to notice the quality of their own work, which my research showed was often a default approach among women. Warming to my subject, I advised participants never to minimize the scope of their contributions by prefacing their observations with a description of their own perceived inadequacies.

During the discussion that followed, one of the participants noted that I had begun my talk by modeling precisely the conduct I was now denouncing. By emphasizing the accidental aspect of my role as expert and my observer status, wasn't I refusing to claim my own achievement?

I started to respond by talking about the objectivity that writing required, but even as I spoke I could hear the defensiveness in my voice. So I stopped mid-course and began instead to explore aloud the ways in which her observations might be true. Doing so gave me a powerful sense of kinship with the women in the room. I was speaking both as an expert—and yes, a leader—*and* as someone who shared their experience, inhibitions, and doubts. As my defenses crumbled, I recognized that my own ambivalence was not serving the women who looked to my work for guidance. Emphasizing it was therefore an indulgence—one that neither I nor those to whom I spoke could afford.

Looking back, I see how that morning changed me. As I walked out into the California sunshine following the event, I resolved to claim my own contribution to the world and accept the mantle of leadership that had been thrust upon me. However inadvertently, I had created the place I now held in the world, and I had a responsibility to receive it with grace. Reluctance would only shortchange those attracted by my message, and undermine any power I had to affect change.

Upon reflection, I recognized that authentic leadership often comes unsolicited, the result of achievements that inspire trust in others. If you put those achievements out in the world, whatever your intention, you need to take responsibility for the possibilities they create. If what you put forth meets a need in the world, you must do whatever you can to help others find a way to fulfill it.

I also began to understand that assuming the mantle of leadership requires not just willingness and expertise, but also the capacity to share in the experience of those who look to you. I could not fully claim my achievement until I recognized that my reluctance to do so was rooted in the same ambivalence and fear that the women I wrote about experienced. My capacity as a leader depended on the paradox of being able to embody the vulnerabilities I sought to address.

QUESTIONS

✣ *How have you journeyed to authenticity in your professional life? In your personal life? Have you taken this journey?*

✣ *What fears have you let go of, or could you let go of, to take this journey?*

✣ *Have you taken, or do you take, responsibility for the possibilities that your achievements have created?*

4   ALAN M. WEBBER

Alan M. Webber was the editorial director of the Harvard Business Review *and cofounding editor of* Fast Company *magazine. Prior to that he worked as an administrative assistant to the Mayor of Portland, Oregon, and special assistant to the U.S. Secretary of Transportation. Most recently he is author of* Rules of Thumb: 52 Truths for Winning at Business Without Losing Your Self *(HarperCollins, 2009).*

Speaking Truth Is Power

The year was 1971. I was twenty-two years old, living in Portland, Oregon, working as an inexperienced, newly hired, wet behind the years administrative assistant to an equally young city commissioner, Neil Goldschmidt. The Vietnam War was still raging, dividing the country and the community. A couple of months before I joined his staff, Commissioner Goldschmidt had introduced a resolution in the city council condemning the war, but the council had refused to act on it. After just a few days working in City Hall it was clear to me that the subject of the war and everything it represented still hung in the air.

The situation was made more complicated by Commissioner Goldschmidt's intention to run for mayor. He was young, he'd served only half of one term on the city council, and he had a very different agenda for the city than the old guard. The sitting mayor had announced his intention to retire, having been plagued by health problems due to old age. The way the city's rules worked, in situations where the mayor was absent or ill, the city council president became mayor pro tem. Commissioner Goldschmidt, it happened, was mayor pro tem.

At that exact moment the opponents of the Vietnam War announced their intention to hold a march through downtown Portland. They applied to the city—represented by the mayor pro tem—for a permit for the march.

The permit request put Commissioner-Mayor Pro Tem-Candidate Goldschmidt in a bind. Before running for office, he'd been a legal aid attorney: how could he turn down a request for a peaceful demonstration? And he'd already shown that he was an opponent of the war himself. The problem was, a previous demonstration had turned violent. A splinter group had broken off from the march, breaking windows and rampaging through downtown. What if that happened again? A second violent anti-war demonstration, marching with a permit signed by Mayor Pro Tem Goldschmidt, could be enough to wipe out my boss's campaign to become the elected mayor.

✿   ✿   ✿

All I was told was that there was a meeting in the conference room and I was supposed to be there.

When I got there I sat down at one end of the long table, near my boss, next to one or two other, more experienced, members of his staff. At the time, given my age and salary, I was buying most of my work clothes from the Junior League Bargain Tree. The re-sell-it shop had a nice assortment of used jackets and suits that made me look a little more presentable when I showed up to work at City Hall each morning.

After the Mayor Pro Tem and his staff were all seated, the other people who'd been invited to the meeting were ushered in.

The police brass came in first—the chief and his top team. They were wearing the full police uniform regalia. There must have been at least six of them. I didn't know any of their names. But looking at them as they filed in and took their places on one side of the table, I felt intimidated by their age, uniforms, authority—their presence.

Then the leaders of the anti-war movement came in. They were all my age. They were wearing jeans and work shirts. They looked the way I looked before I got my job in City Hall. They sat down across the table from the cops.

The meeting began. My boss explained the purpose: in light of the violence and damage that had taken place during the last march, he was putting the onus on the demonstrators. What assurances could they give that, if he gave them a permit, they would be able to control the crowd?

The demonstrators shot right back. What happened to freedom of assembly? Free speech? Besides, it wasn't their job to prevent splinter groups from breaking off—wasn't that what the cops were supposed to do? For good measure, they lobbed a taunt at the police: They had inside information that the violent demonstrators were either stoolies for the police or actual off-duty cops out to discredit the peace movement.

That set things off for a while. The two sides exchanged accusations and insults, denials and refutations. Finally, my boss brought things back to his original question: What were the demonstrators prepared to do to prevent another violent outbreak? How were they going to police themselves?

They were holding training sessions at a local community center, one of them volunteered. They were recruiting marshals and training them to keep the crowd under control. They didn't want another outbreak of violence any more than we did, said one of the spokesmen.

The police were quick to pounce. Where was the community center? When were the training sessions? How many people would be there? What kind of techniques were they teaching? And, finally, could the police come and observe?

Absolutely not, the answer came back. There was no way the police could observe! That was a form of intimidation, said one demonstrator. The police would probably bring cameras and photograph everyone.

No cameras, the police said; they just wanted to observe. They hoped to be able to work with the marshals, if something happened.

The demonstrators were adamant: No cops at their meeting. No cops, no cooperation.

I hadn't said a word up until then. I was too young and too green. A few years before, I'd been the one organizing demonstrations in college, driving to Washington, DC, as part of the MOBE. But maybe it was that fact, that experience, that gave me a flash of insight: Though he hadn't said it, I knew for certain what the anti-war leader was thinking.

I looked him in the eye and said, "You don't want the cops to come because they might not live up to your stereotype?"

The room became absolutely silent.

It was instantly clear that I'd spoken the unspoken truth. It's hard to have an enemy when they don't perform to your stereotypical expectations, when they turn out to be ok.

❧   ❧   ❧

What happened next?

The police went to the meeting where the marshals were trained, without cameras, without incident.

The demonstrators got their permit to march.

The march went off without a problem.

The city commissioner got elected mayor.

I became one of his most trusted staffers and continued to base my relationship with him on speaking the truth as I saw it.

Portland, Oregon, became one of the most livable cities in the United States.

QUESTIONS

�֍   *What is the risk of speaking up or asking the hard, unasked question in a meeting? What is the risk of not doing it?*

✖   *Do you speak up, dissent, raise unwelcome questions? Do you encourage or reward others when they do?*

✖   *What do you do to avoid groupthink in your organization?*

✖   *How would you describe your organization's culture? Fearful? Courageous? Risk-taking? Cautious? Who sets the culture—and what would it take to reset it to make it more honest, more candid, and more self-aware?*

Key Learning Points:
Lessons on Leadership

Learning to live our own lives effectively often provides the most powerful lessons on leadership. After all, if we cannot be leaders for ourselves, how can we be leaders for others? And for others to trust us as leaders, they must know us; they must see our true selves. That means that we must know and be willing to reveal our true selves. Authenticity requires us to be true to ourselves as well as to others—true in our conversations, our behaviors, and our intentions. Significant events or individuals in our lives can enable us to find our true voice and feelings, and getting to our personal truths can be a valuable journey toward leadership. Nancy Dixon, in her book *Perspectives on Dialogue*, suggests how difficult this is in organizational life: "I believe that people long for a more authentic kind of interaction with their co-workers but they are not sure that it is possible, or even if their longing is legitimate. Work is not generally thought of as a place where you are supposed to get your own needs met. Thus, people come to accept what they believe to be inevitable: that they must leave a part of themselves at home when they come to work."

After reading the preceding chapters, consider your own journey to authenticity and leadership:

✢   *In your life's story, are you your own author? What kind of life are you writing?*

✢   *What has been your experience regarding the discovery of your authentic self?*

✢   *Were there key players or events that were significant?*

✢   *What are some situations in which it has been difficult to be authentic as a leader?*

✢   *What is the downside to not being true to yourself and to others?*

✢   *How do you nurture authenticity in your relationships?*

CROSSROADS AND CHOICES

PETER BLOCK
Everything Counts

CHARLES GARFIELD
The Dancing Toll Taker

WILLIAM BRIDGES
Living "As If"

ROBERT ROSEN
Learning Journeys as Great Teachers

5 PETER BLOCK

*Peter Block is an author, consultant, and citizen of
Cincinnati, Ohio. His work is about empowerment, stewardship, chosen accountability, and community building.
Peter's books include* Flawless Consulting, Stewardship,
The Empowered Manager, Freedom and Accountability at Work *with Peter Koestenbaum,* The Answer to
How Is Yes, Community: The Structure of Belonging,
and The Abundant Community *with John McKnight.
The books are about ways to create workplaces and communities that work for all. They offer an alternative to the
patriarchal beliefs that dominate our culture. He is a
partner in Designed Learning, a training company that
offers workshops designed by Peter to build the skills
outlined in his books. Peter serves on several boards and
advisory groups, which include Cincinnati Public Radio
and Elementz, a Hip Hop Center for youth. Peter began
A Small Group, a civic engagement network whose work
is to change the narrative within and about our cities. He
can be reached at (860) 572-0346 or pbi@att.net*

Everything Counts

  I can't think of anything that has had an impact on my life that
hasn't changed my work, and I can't think of anything significant that
has happened in my work that hasn't changed my life. Personal changes,

changes in thinking, and changes in practice are all one and the same. There have been several events in my work that caused my thinking to shift in a major way.

I first started in organization development in my late twenties working with T-groups. For almost five years I worked under the belief that the point was to always get it right. I believed that when I spoke, I should speak what was true and well thought out, and when I did my work, I should have a clear goal in mind. I was anxious and ambitious, and I wanted to be somebody.

After leading groups for a number of years, I began to participate in weekend Gestalt workshops. Up to that point, I had focused on being a good trainer, consultant, father, husband, and neighbor. I was meeting the external requirements of what the world expected of me and of what I expected of myself. From Gestalt work, I got the expression "Who you are is everything." What defines you as a person is not what you do, what you did, or how you present yourself. I came to believe that what defines people is their capacity to understand and give expression to their own experience. My focus switched from viewing life on the basis of accomplishment to that of experience.

This learning redefined how I worked. Instead of asking people, "What would constitute an agreement?" or, "How do we resolve this issue?" I would ask them questions about what they were experiencing. I discovered that resolution of conflict comes from people being able to express their own feelings and their own needs in the face of another. Making agreements and setting goals without building upon the feelings of the parties involved is empty, because it does not consider the vulnerabilities of our own humanity. What counts is an individual's capacity to express or state who he or she is, not so much the ability to set and reach a specific goal.

The second major turning point occurred when I was thirty-six. I read Tim Gallwey's *Inner Game of Tennis*. Using the game of tennis as a metaphor, Gallwey offered stunning insights about performing and learning. His basic stance is that awareness, body awareness in the case of tennis, is the antidote to self-doubt and self-judgment. This turned on a lightbulb in my brain and gave me a way to become more connected to the world and to myself.

I was also greatly affected by his notion that in terms of our spiritual and philosophical lives, we have within us the wisdom to answer all our questions. Learning is a process of rediscovering what we already know. This caused me to question the purpose of skill training. Why do we prescribe behavior and ask people to practice, copy, and imitate? Doesn't this demean the human spirit and destroy what is part of the individual? To prescribe to people what they should learn or how they should perform is to keep them from truly learning.

For example, I used to hate talking in front of people. I'm an introvert. I would fight myself when I gave a presentation. I tried hard to be dynamic and charismatic, to fulfill the image of the ideal presenter that was in my head. Finally I said, "To hell with it. I'm never going to be a good speaker. Why don't I just stand up and say something?" And as a result I became a good presenter. I stopped trying so hard. I understood that my anxiety was about finding my own voice. It was a sign of being alive, so get on with it.

The third life-changing event occurred when I was forty. I was in Stockholm running an Inner Game of Tennis clinic, and I happened to go to a lecture by Peter Koestenbaum. Peter, a professor of philosophy, talked about a deep part of the structure of life in which each person has to deal with fundamental issues, such as purpose, destiny, aloneness, and mortality—issues I had never taken seriously. In an audience of 300 I sat paralyzed. I don't know if half of what he said even registered, but just the idea that destiny and purpose were everybody's issue stunned me.

I left Peter's lecture with the simple wish that he would not visit my workshop to witness the superficiality and shallowness that would be visible for all to see. Luckily he came in late, and afterward I told him how touched I was by what he had said. asked him if I could visit him, and told him I needed help in understanding what he was talking about.

I visited Peter at his home in San Jose and explained to him that about every seven years, my life seems to dissemble and I find myself having to start over again. In response to this, Peter asked me, "What is your destiny?" I replied that I didn't know. The questions of choosing greatness and purpose, as well as the fact that reaffirming your life mattered, were huge issues for me. I attended every lecture of his I could, and every time I was in California I would visit him. It was another ten years before I understood what he was talking about.

Peter's influence helped me create all the work I did with empowerment. I became a translator of Peter's ideas into the workplace. There are questions that are still unanswered, but the important point is that I know they are there. The question of "calling" is part of that. Each of us needs to find out what we're here for and pursue it. We each have a vision of greatness, whether or not we want to accept it.

People ask me sometimes what impact I've had on people over the last thirty years. The answer is none. Maybe at my best I've touched other people's lives as Gestalt workshops, Tim Gallwey, and Peter Koestenbaum have touched mine, but I don't give them credit for my life. They have added tremendous value. Others give a gift, but in the end each of us chooses and is responsible for our own life.

QUESTIONS

✢ *What courage is required at this point in our life?*

✢ *How do we reclaim the freedom we have so easily given away?*

6 CHARLES GARFIELD

Dr. Charles Garfield is author of the widely acclaimed Peak
Performance *trilogy:* Peak Performers, Team Management, *and* Second to None. *His books focus on high performing individuals, teams, and organizations, respectively,
and have established Dr. Charles Garfield as one of America's leading authorities on high achievement. Simply put, the
trilogy constitutes a blueprint for leaders and teams pres-
sured to continuously improve while doing more with less.*

The Dancing Toll Taker

If you have ever gone through a tollbooth, you know that your
relationship to the person in the booth is not the most intimate you'll
ever have. It is one of life's frequent non-encounters: You hand over
some money; you might get change; you drive off.

I have been through every one of the seventeen tollbooths on the
Oakland–San Francisco Bay Bridge on thousands of occasions, and I
never had an exchange with a toll taker that was worth remembering
until late one morning in 1984.

I was headed for lunch in San Francisco as I drove toward one of the
booths. I heard loud rock music. It sounded like a party or a Michael Jack-
son concert. I looked around—no other cars with their windows open, no
sound trucks. I looked at the tollbooth. Inside it, a man was dancing.

"What are you doing?" I asked.

"I'm having a party," he said.

"What about the rest of these people?" I looked over at other booths; nothing moving there.

"They're not invited."

I had a dozen other questions for him, but somebody in a big hurry to get somewhere started punching his horn behind me. I drove off, but I made a note to myself: find this guy again. There's something in his eye that says there's magic in his tollbooth.

Months later I did find him again, still with the loud music, still having a party. Again I asked, "What are you doing?"

He said, "I remember you from the last time. I'm still dancing. I'm having the same party."

I said, "Look. What about the rest of these people?"

He said, "Stop. What do those look like to you?" He pointed down the row of tollbooths.

"They look like tollbooths."

"Noooo, imagination!"

I said, "Okay, I give up. What do they look like to you?"

He said, "Vertical coffins."

"What are you talking about?"

"I can prove it. At 8:30 every morning, live people get in. Then they die for eight hours. At 4:30, like Lazarus from the dead, they reemerge and go home. For eight hours, the brain is on hold, dead on the job. Going through the motions."

I was amazed. This guy had developed a philosophy, a mythology about his job. I could not help asking the next question: "Why is it different for you? You're having a good time."

He looked at me. "I knew you were going to ask that," he said. "I'm going to be a dancer someday." He pointed to the administration building. "My bosses are in there, and they're paying for my training."

Sixteen people dead on the job, and the seventeenth, in precisely the same situation, figures out a way to live. That man was having a party where you and I would probably not last three days. The boredom! He and I had lunch later, and he said, "I don't understand why anybody would think my job is boring. I have a corner office, glass on all sides. I can see the Golden Gate bridge, San Francisco, the Berkeley hills; half the Western world vacations here, and I just stroll in every day and practice dancing."

What is the essential skill that, when seventeen human beings walk into their offices and sixteen of them get vertical coffins, allows one of them to have a party? Mission. Purpose. Some people do the same jobs as everybody else but have an unusual sense of mission; they enjoy it, and they have the energy to achieve at high levels.

The dancing toll taker had been given no special jobs, no change in the conditions that limited life for everyone else in the booths. Yet he had found a mission, and thereby he had discovered the will and the way to use the conditions of his job to support his mission. He had found what Archimedes said he would need, along with his lever, to move the Earth: a place to stand.

He had found that place we might call a zone of peak performance, where he can align his personal mission with the specific demands of a job and the overall environment and objectives of an organization. It is a place for major productive impact, an optimal leverage point for one's abilities. I don't know if the toll taker has found the audience he was looking for, but I do know that when one observes peak performers long enough, it becomes increasingly clear that one of their major talents is finding such a place of personal power.

And why not? Their desire for a place to stand is based on keen appreciation of leverage, on the knowledge that it is from such a location that their mission has its best chance to succeed. When they have the abilities that a job requires and work in an environment that supports what they do, they encounter relatively little resistance.

Moreover, when a job provides the vehicle for accomplishing one's mission, when one's place to stand supports any task that may arise, one develops confidence in one's ability to complete the current mission and manage anything else that comes along.

What if the congruence is not there, and there is no solid place to stand, and you still have your job to do? Then it is tempting to force oneself, through superhuman acts of will, to overcome limitations in any of the three areas. We all know how hard it is to try to lift the weight with little leverage. People can be courageous and tenacious, and often do try to do the job even though they know they aren't in the right spot. People often know they are not positioned correctly for their best efforts, and it weakens their willingness to take a stand and their ability to manage what occurs along the way.

The place to stand suggests an opposite to the Peter Principle and its tart notion of people being promoted to their level of incompetence. I am talking about positioning ourselves for considerable competence, arriving at a place from which all things seem possible. And whether our specific road to achievement leads to Wall Street, Silicon Valley, or Damascus, we could, with tongue in cheek, call it the Paul Principle.

People who locate their place to stand like what they are doing. They feel a commitment to it. They feel themselves growing, learning, and experiencing through it. They have found not only their mission, but a firm standpoint, a situation, one might say an optimal context from which to make it happen. They see concrete results emerging from what they do. They, not just other people, recognize the contribution they are making.

QUESTIONS

✢ *Are you one of the sixteen people dead on the job, or are you like the seventeenth toll taker?*

✢ *Where is your place of personal power?*

✢ *Do you recognize the contribution you are making? Do you feel yourself growing, learning, and experiencing through what you do?*

7

WILLIAM BRIDGES

William Bridges, founder of William Bridges and Associates, has written, spoken, and consulted on the subject of transition and how organizations and individuals can deal with change and transition successfully. He has written ten books, including Transitions, Managing Transitions, The Way of Transition, *and* JobShift. *He was named by* The Wall Street Journal *as one of the top ten independent executive development presenters in the country. Bridges' clients have included AT&T, Intel, Hewlett-Packard, Amoco, and Procter & Gamble, as well as the Veterans Administration and the U.S. Department of Energy and the Department of Human Services. Educated in the humanities at Harvard, Columbia, and Brown universities, Bridges was a professor of American literature before changing careers at age forty. Bridges is also a past president of the Association for Humanistic Psychology.*

Living "As If"

When I was about forty years old, I was teaching literature at the college level. I had a sabbatical coming up, and during this sabbatical I spent a great deal of time researching the psychology of literature and how literature affects people. I had no idea what would come of this research, but I found it fascinating. When I tried to put my findings into words, the writing seemed very dead, and yet the subject was very alive to me. I didn't know why the ideas seemed to die when I wrote them down.

One day I was reading a section of what I had written to my wife. She said, "This is so academic."

"I am an academic," I replied. "Give me a break."

Then she explained what she meant: "You're talking a lot about what other people think. What do you think?"

I gave a weasely answer, something like, "I'm just showing where my thoughts came from." But it rankled me to have her point out that I could talk about what other people said was so, but I never said what I thought was so.

The next day I started writing as though I knew what was true. But I had to write "as if," because at that time my mind was shaped by the academic, what-are-your-sources culture. As long as I could play a game with myself and say I'm only writing as if I know something, then I could playact my way into a kind of writing, which subsequently became speaking, that was more like bearing witness to a reality than it was like reporting on other people's perceptions of a reality.

I can't say how much of my life since that time has come straight from those days and how much I owe to acting as though my perceptions had some validity. At the time I was doing this, I was primarily teaching nineteenth-century U.S. writers, particularly Ralph Waldo Emerson, Henry David Thoreau, and Walt Whitman. All three were useful for demonstrating what I had learned, but a line from Emerson* stuck with me. He said, in effect, "Don't use quotations; tell me what you know."

I decided that I would take Emerson's point seriously. Emerson had been a minister and had resigned from that prestigious position. His wife died of tuberculosis not long after they were married, and in the period after her death, Emerson made a trip to Europe. Evidently, he

---

*All Emerson quotations are paraphrased.

just couldn't preach anymore. Emerson had had doubts about conventional Christianity, and his wife's death pulled out the last props from under him. While in Europe Emerson wrote in his journal, "I wonder if I have the courage to look at every part of the world in its relation to myself, and to accept nothing on secondhand knowledge." He said, "That's what I'd like to do." And he built his career on that idea.

In Emerson's well-known essay "Self-Reliance," he said that "imitation is suicide" and "Say what is true for you and every heart will respond to that iron string." So Emerson and Thoreau—who also did what was true for him—and Whitman became my guides and have been my guides ever since.

When Emerson was about my present age, he said, "I've been reflecting recently on why I don't have any followers. A lot of other people who have written less than I have, have all kinds of followers." He continued, "I decided the other day that it is because those other people were trying to bring people to them while I've been trying to bring people to themselves." I would want Emerson to know that it worked for me—that his work didn't bring me to Emerson; his work brought me to myself. This is my goal when I work with people and organizations, and I think I picked it up from him all those years ago—to bring people to themselves.

I am so grateful that Emerson's words have allowed me to be who I really am.

QUESTIONS

☧ *If you were to speak from your own heart and say what is most deeply true for you, what would you be saying these days?*

☧ *And if you were able to build a work life based on those personal truths, what would it be? What kind of work would you be doing? With whom?*

8 ROBERT ROSEN

Dr. Robert Rosen is an internationally recognized psychologist, bestselling author, researcher, and business advisor to world-class companies. He is founder and CEO of Healthy Companies International located in Arlington, Virginia, and has spent twenty years advising and studying top executives, working in all three sectors of the economy—business, government, and nonprofit. Each year he speaks to thousands of executives worldwide and appears regularly in international media, including The Financial Times, The New York Times, BusinessWeek, Fortune, *and* The Washington Post. *Recent books by Dr. Rosen are* Just Enough Anxiety: The Hidden Driver of Business Success *and* The Catalyst.

Learning Journeys as Great Teachers

 My story revolves around three incidents that happened early in my career. They each showed me how people shed light or cast darkness on those around them. From these experiences I became a student of healthy leadership and made a personal commitment to shed as much light as possible, and to help and celebrate others who do the same.

The first incident occurred while I was working in the Department of Psychiatry at George Washington University School of Medicine. I had just finished my doctoral training in clinical psychology and was treating executive families. One day a mother brought her teenage son to see me. He was having drug and conduct disorder problems. The father was apparently too busy at work and could not come to the appointment. I later found out that this successful businessman was running both himself and his company into the ground. After a few weeks of therapy, they terminated treatment.

Several years later I ran into the mother. She told me that her husband's company had gone bankrupt, and when he developed an alcohol problem, she divorced him. Their son was being treated in a psychiatric hospital. This episode affected me deeply. It was my first experience dealing with the impact of an executive who had cast incredible darkness on everyone he touched.

The second incident occurred while working with the Herman Miller Company, a progressive furniture manufacturer in Zeeland, Michigan. I was excited at the opportunity because it was one of my first consulting jobs with a Fortune 500 company. On the first day there, I found myself in the company auditorium preparing for a meeting. While waiting, I watched a woman very carefully put chairs in a row: she was absolutely meticulous. So impressed by her display, I said, "You look like you really care about what you're doing."

She replied, "The person who runs this company *really cares* about my life and my family."

I eventually got to meet "the person who runs this company," Max Depree. This was one of my first interviews with a CEO who cast light on those around him, most of the time. What a comparison.

Several months later I experienced darkness once again. I was at a conference and during a break got up to get a cup of coffee. I found myself standing next to the CEO of a large Fortune 100 insurance company. I was young and curious at the time, and started up a conversation. In mid-sentence, completely ignoring what I had to say, he walked off with his coffee. It was as if I was a spoon on the table. That was the first and only time I had ever been totally dismissed as a person. And I understood in raw detail the powerful effect of egotistical leadership.

From these and other experiences I grew to understand the power of leadership, both as a liberator of human spirit and destroyer of human dignity. Soon after the spoon incident, I made a personal commitment to do my best (I don't always do it) to cast as much light as possible on other people. Part of that pledge is to understand people and their companies at a deep level, and to celebrate people doing the same. Rather than focus on the pathologies of people, which as a trained psychologist it is easy to do, I focus on what make people strong, good, vital, and productive. Since that first experience thirty years ago, I have interviewed and/or advised more than three hundred CEOs in forty countries. As a CEO advisor, speaker, and author, I have always tried to tell the truth about the human side of business, make a business case for why it matters, and tell stories of healthy, successful leaders making a difference around the world.

QUESTIONS

✢   *How do you shed light on the people around you? What in your personality and behavior brings out people's personal best?*

✢   *How do you cast darkness? What prejudices, blind spots, and shortcomings undermine people, and ultimately yourself?*

Key Learning Points: Crossroads and Choices

Robert Frost said it best. That fork in the road presents itself almost every day, and we must make a choice. Our natural tendency may be to take a well-worn path, but we can experiment and explore the new. All paths can lead to learning and personal growth, and in fact, sometimes it is the more mundane choices that have the most impact. Our decisions involve what kind of mood to be in, how to treat people, how to treat ourselves, and what to do with our lives. Big choices are often so difficult that they become painful, but of course we all know that not to decide is a decision in itself.

After reading the preceding chapters, consider the following questions about your life crossroads:

* *What have been major decision points in your life? What prompted one of these decisions?*

* *What have been your experiences with making pivotal choices that worked out well? Describe one that didn't turn out well.*

* *How can you help others learn to make better choices and to accept the choices they make?*

* *Who has helped you make the best decisions, and how have these people been influences?*

* *How do you make choices about your life? Do you involve others? Do you labor silently?*

* *What have you learned about your choices that will be helpful to tell others?*

LEADING, LEARNING, AND TEACHING

STEPHEN R. COVEY
Shaping Experiences

JAMES M. KOUZES
Teaching and Training

JAMES BELASCO
The Learner's Point of View

PAUL HERSEY
Standing on the Shoulders of Giants

HOMA BAHRAMI
Nurturing Learning Partnerships

9

STEPHEN R. COVEY

*Stephen Covey is an internationally respected leadership
authority, family expert, and teacher. He is an organizational consultant, founder of the former Covey Leadership
Center, and vice chairman of Franklin Covey Company.
He has made teaching principle-centered living and
principle-centered leadership his life's work. Covey is the
author of* The 7 Habits of Highly Effective People, *chosen by readers of* Chief Executive *magazine as the
most influential book of the twentieth century;* Principle-
Centered Leadership; *and* Living the 7 Habits; *and
coauthor of* First Things First. *He has also been featured
as one of* Time *magazine's twenty-five most influential
Americans. He has received the Thomas More College
Medallion for continuing service to humanity, the Toast-
masters International Top Speaker Award, and several
honorary doctorates.*

Shaping Experiences

I've had many powerfully shaping experiences in my life. In this
chapter, I share six of them with you with the hope that my learning
journey might be helpful to you.

First, when I was a university student, I had a speech professor
who was one of the finest professional speakers in the country. Most

weeks, he would travel and give two or more speeches somewhere in the country.

At the end of the semester, I asked him, "If you were to do it all over again, what would you do differently?" He said, "I would institutionalize my work—build an organization, so there could be follow-through on my teaching and speaking."

I didn't know it at the time, but his comment powerfully influenced my decision later in life to supplement my teaching with outside speaking and consulting experiences and eventually to leave my post at the university and start my own company.

Second, while teaching at the university, I met a visiting professor, Dr. Walter Gong from San Jose, California. He taught a class for faculty entitled "How to Improve Your Teaching." It lasted one entire semester. The essence of his program was this great principle: *The best way to get people to learn is to turn them into teachers.* In other words, you learn the material best when you teach it.

I immediately started to apply that principle in my work and at home. When I first started university teaching, my classes only had about fifteen to thirty students. When I started applying Dr. Gong's principle, I found that I could effectively teach many more students; in fact, some of my classes were packed with nearly one thousand students, and yet the students' performance and test scores actually went up. Why? When you teach you simply learn better. Every student becomes a teacher, and every teacher a student.

Now, the common paradigm is that the teacher-student ratio is critical—fewer students means higher-quality teaching. But if you turn your students into teachers, you gain leverage. You move the fulcrum over. Also, when you teach, you implicitly commit socially to live what you teach. In this way learning by teaching beautifully illustrates the second great commandment.

Third, after teaching business executives the importance of having a mission statement and involving members of the organization in its development, I decided to involve my own immediate family in the development of a family mission statement. My mother; my wife, Sandra;

and all nine of our children were deeply involved in this activity over a period of eight months. Eventually, we produced this statement: "The mission of our family is to create a nurturing place of faith, order, truth, love, happiness, and relaxation, and to provide opportunity for every person to become responsibly independent and effectively interdependent, in order to serve worthy purposes in society, through understanding and living the gospel of Jesus Christ."

There are four parts to our family mission statement: (1) the characteristics of our home; (2) the effects on the individual; (3) the purpose of contribution, of making a difference; and (4) the source of the power. We put that mission statement up in our home, and we examine ourselves against it every week in a family meeting. How well do we measure up to this? We found that in many ways we fail. But we constantly come back to it, much like a pilot might fly a plane off track 90 percent of the time, making small deviations and course corrections based on feedback from the environment, but eventually arriving at the destination. We found that at any given point in time, we might be off track, but the key to progress was having a clear sense of destination and direction, and continually returning to course. The process of developing a family mission statement inevitably created personal mission statements with us all. I can't begin to describe the immense positive effect that these personal and family statements have had on our family and now on our grandchildren. In our own family, we find that "adopting" other families, particularly those at risk, is one of the best ways to fulfill our mission of trying to make a difference by participating in worthy causes.

Fourth, another extremely powerful shaping experience was my doctoral work, where I reviewed two hundred years (1776 to 1976) of the so-called "success" literature of our country. I found that for the first 150 years, the focus was primarily on what I call "the character ethic"—on principles and natural laws that are timeless, universal, and self-evident. Then, over the next fifty years, the focus started to shift toward what I call "the personality ethic"—a focus primarily on image and personality-based influence techniques. And, over the last thirty-five years, since my doctoral work, there has been an even more pronounced separation from the character ethic. Even though considerable lip service is constantly paid to it, the primary focus of our business and success literature is on appearances, politics, financial gain, and application of new techniques and technologies.

Fifth, the thrust of my background and training has taught me this: *The key to human influence is first to be influenced—first understand, before seeking to be understood.* People are only open to influence when they feel understood. I find in my consulting and training with client organizations that once I understand how people think, what their burning issues are, their deep concerns, I can adapt my approach and gain greater influence, particularly if my approach is based on principles, not just on short-term entertainment or good stories. If I seek first to understand and even have my thinking and my message influenced by their feelings and concerns, I find people are much more open to my influence.

I then try to teach people timeless principles, a new way of thinking—something that can powerfully influence behavior over time—and leave them with a sense of responsibility and a personal commitment to apply these principles in both their personal and professional lives. This way you have a long-lasting impact and influence. When your students or clients get grounded in principles, they cease looking to you for answers. They cease needing external motivation. They become increasingly independent and capable of thinking their own thoughts, coming up with their own solutions and applications, within this new frame of reference. As the Eastern expression goes, "When you give a man a fish, you feed him for a day; when you teach a man to fish, you feed him for a lifetime."

In the Middle Ages, some doctors tried to heal people through bloodletting. The theory was that the bad stuff is in the blood, and so you let it out. If this didn't work, and you didn't question the theory, what would you do? You'd let out more blood, faster. You might get into TQM on bloodletting or you might go into Team Building by putting people in the mountains and letting them do free falls off cliffs. This way, when they return to the bloodletting unit, they will do it with more spirit of cooperation. You might teach them positive thinking techniques, so that they exude positive energy. You might even put the patients into smile training, so that they exude positive energy while you do the bloodletting. But the problem is with the theory, not in the attitude or behavior. When Pasteur and other scientists discovered the germ theory, the fundamental cause of disease, we understood for the first time why pregnant women at the time preferred to be delivered by midwives, rather than doctors, because midwives were cleaner. In war, more people were dying from staph diseases behind the front lines than from bullets. The germ theory explained so much; everything was organized differently. That's the power of a paradigm—a way of thinking, a way of understanding reality.

The power of a paradigm of principles that are changeless, universal, self-evident, and self-validated is that people inwardly know that they are valid and true. For example, one self-evident principle is this: *You can't talk yourself out of problems that you behave yourself into.* If you hope to produce a culture of trust in a dynamic marketplace with world-class expectations and standards, you've got to have trustworthiness. If you hope to have people who are grounded in a set of principles so that they (on their own initiative) network with other people, empathizing and creating new win-win alternatives; if you hope to develop a competence to accommodate the new realities, to cultivate your own immune system, so that no matter what comes, you have the capability to adapt, you need to build into your structures and systems the principles and processes of involvement, accountability, responsibility, and commitment over time.

There is a growing awareness that if we are to solve the massive social problems we face, we need a different mind-set and skill set, based on principles, based on the restoration of the character ethic. You can't fake integrity. It is the integration of your own personality and your relationship with other people.

Sixth, by teaching the *7 Habits and Principle-Centered Leadership* in cultures and nations all over the world, I have learned that these principles truly are universal. If you can get enough people interacting deeply and sincerely as they develop their mission statements, and if you can get them to reflect and listen to their conscience and to ask deep questions, they will come up with the same basic mission statement.

They will use different words, but their missions will deal with the four dimensions of life: to live, to love, to learn, and to leave a legacy. "To live" has to do with the physical and economic dimension. "To love" has to do with relationships, with respect and dignity. "To learn" deals with the constant need for growth and development, for bench marking against world-class standards. And "to leave a legacy" is to matter, to make a difference, to contribute.

To make the point about universal principles, I often tell the following story:

On a dark and stormy night, the captain of a ship at sea received a frantic wake-up call.

"Captain, captain, wake up."

"What is it?"

"Sorry to wake you, sir, but we have a real problem."

"What is it?"

"There's a ship in our sea-lane, several miles away, and they refuse to move."

"Tell them to move."

"We have, sir. They just won't move."

"I'll tell them! Move starboard 20 degrees."

The signal returned, "Move starboard yourself, 20 degrees."

"I can't believe this," roared the captain. "Who is this joker? Does he know I'm the captain? Tell him who I am!"

The signal goes out, "This is Captain Horatio Hornblower, the 26th, commanding you to move starboard 20 degrees, at once."

The signal returns, "This is seaman Carl Jones, the 3rd, commanding you to move starboard 20 degrees, at once."

"I can't believe this. What arrogance. We're a battleship. We could blow them out of the water. Let him know who we are!"

"This is the mighty *Missouri*, flagship of the seventh fleet."

The signal returned, "This is the lighthouse."

Though I've paraphrased it a bit, it's a true story, published in the *Naval Proceedings Manual*. They actually interpreted a lighthouse as a ship. Principles are like lighthouses. You do not break them—you only break yourself against them. Foundational principles represent "true north." Because, it doesn't make any difference where you are, the compass will always point to true north, to natural laws and principles. You will also find on the compass another indicator, called the "direction of travel." That stands for your behavior, motive, attitude, direction, and sense of destination. If you wanted to go 90 degrees east, you'd put the direction of travel at that mark and follow.

I encourage you to study your "direction of travel" in your personal life and in your organization and check for alignment between your direction and true-north principles. Apply this test to your personal life, your interpersonal relations, your managerial work, your leadership, and your organization. By doing this regularly, you will start to build a culture that aligns itself with principles and with a common vision and mission.

The alignment process is tough duty because many traditions develop in the way the organization recruits, trains, rewards, compensates, and reinforces people. But over time you build the principles of respect and trust and alignment with natural laws throughout the culture.

The real challenge, I find, is to live in alignment with your personal mission statement. For me, it is a constant struggle, even with everything that I teach. I'm grateful for 360-degree feedback in our organization and for feedback from my wife, children, and conscience. I believe God, the Father of us all, is the source of our conscience, and that is why conscience gives us an accurate sense of whether or not our lives are in alignment with those natural laws and principles upon which everything that endures is based.

If you plant a Chinese bamboo tree, you see no growth at all for four years. Finally, a tiny shoot appears. But in the fifth year, this special species of the bamboo tree grows eighty feet! Likewise, people, families, and organizations that build on universal, timeless principles will grow impressively on a strong foundation.

We can make such significant difference in the lives of other people. I know many great teachers and trainers who are doing just that—who are impacting communities, associations, schools, children, students, and families. If we focus on everything in our society but neglect the family, we are simply straightening deck chairs on the *Titanic*. The nature of the work we do as teachers is so significant. T. S. Eliot once said, "We must never cease from exploring. In the end, all of our exploring will be to arrive where we began and to know the place for the first time."

We already know this. This material is basically common sense, but it still is not common practice. We constantly need to upgrade our skills and abilities, and to nurture our desires—and those of others—to live by the character ethic. I echo the words of T. R. Chardin: "We are not human beings having a spiritual experience; we are spiritual beings having a human experience."

All six of these shaping forces have encouraged and empowered me to constantly strive to build for the long term—to build a life, a marriage, a family, and an organization on the foundation of correct principles and the character ethic.

QUESTIONS

✢ *If you were to live your life all over again, what would you do differently?*

✢ *What is your mission statement?*

✢ *If you study your "direction of travel," do you find your personal and professional lives are aligned with your personal mission statement?*

✢ *Why or why not?*

10   JAMES M. KOUZES

*Jim is the Dean's Executive Professor of Leadership,
Leavey School of Business, Santa Clara University, and
the coauthor with Barry Posner of the bestselling and
award-winning book* The Leadership Challenge, *now in
its fourth edition with more than 1.8 million copies sold
and translations into twenty-two different languages. Jim
and Barry are also the coauthors of more than thirty other
books and workbooks, including the* Leadership Practices
Inventory, *the bestselling off-the-shelf leadership assess-
ment in the world. In 2009 they were the recipients of the
American Society for Training and Development (ASTD)
Distinguished Contribution to Workplace Learning and
Performance Award.* The Wall Street Journal *has cited
Jim as one of the top ten independent executive educators
in the United States.*

Teaching and Training

I needed a job. It was the summer of 1969 and I'd just returned
to the United States after spending two years serving in Eskişehir,
Turkey, with the Peace Corps. I was twenty-four, still full of the six-
ties' passion to make a difference, but out of work. I'd taught English
as a second language and I'd grown to love learners and learning. Before college I'd toyed with becoming a football player, a minister, an

architect, or a Foreign Service officer, but a persistent voice inside kept telling me to teach. By the time I'd completed my Peace Corps service as a teacher of English as a second language, I was certain I belonged in the classroom.

My search for a teaching job proved fruitless. While I'd been a secondary teacher for two years, no school system in the United States would accept that experience in lieu of a teaching credential. So I turned my attention to finding a community service job in one of the Johnson administration's war on poverty programs. With the help of my dad—a dedicated career civil servant in Washington, DC, where I grew up—I got an interview with the Community Program Training Institute. The institute was in need of some young, eager, and inexpensive talent to provide management and interpersonal skills training to employees of the newly founded Community Action Agencies. I got a job with the southwestern region, riding the circuit throughout Texas, Arkansas, Louisiana, Oklahoma, and New Mexico, spreading the gospel and building skills of effective human relations.

I didn't know much about management back then—except for what my dad would tell us over the dinner table—but I had had the opportunity to experience some of the best interpersonal skills training in the world while preparing for the Peace Corps. The National Training Laboratories (NTL), the pioneer of T-groups, played a major role in the Peace Corps' cross-cultural training, and I'd had the benefit of being exposed to their methods beginning in 1967. I was hungry to conduct some of that kind of training myself.

Whatever my new colleagues and I lacked in practical experience, we made up for in energy, enthusiasm, and a strong desire to serve others. Our new employer was also wise enough to understand how important early world-class training was in preparing its new recruits, so they hired the very best to put us through the paces. It wasn't long before I was hooked, and I began the lifelong adventure that has been my career.

In the process of training, I met some of the most seasoned NTL professionals in the business. One of them was Fred Margolis. Fred was a student of Malcolm Knowles, the father of the theory and method of adult learning known as *andragogy*. Fred was a master, and he taught me a lesson in the early 1970s that has shaped everything I've done as an educator since then.

I was doing some work in Washington, DC, and after a day of training, Fred and I met at an Italian restaurant for dinner. During our dinner, Fred asked me this question: "Jim, what's the best way to learn something?" Since I'd been extensively involved in experiential learning I confidently told Fred the obvious: "The best way to learn something is to experience it yourself."

"No," Fred responded. "The best way to learn something is to teach it to somebody else!" Fred's correction hit me right between the cerebral hemispheres. It was one of those aha moments I will never forget. Suddenly I had a whole new understanding of what it meant to teach and learn. The act of teaching is an act of learning—the deepest kind of learning. You've probably felt the impact of this yourself whenever you've been asked to teach others, whether you're a subject matter expert or a novice.

The moment you're asked to teach you start to think, study, worry, and prepare. In the process you become consumed by learning. You know you're on the line. You're going to have to perform live in front of others and you better know your stuff. You've got to learn at a deeper level. The late management guru Peter Drucker revealed that this was one of the five most important leadership lessons he learned from one of his mentors early in his career. "People learn the most," Drucker observed, "when teaching others. My third employer was the youngest of three senior partners of a bank. Once a week or so he would sit down with me and talk about the way he saw the world. In the end, I think he learned more than I did from our little talks."

That lesson—the best way to learn something is to teach it to someone else—has shaped my style more profoundly than any other lesson on learning. It's become a mantra, and I recite it many times a day. It inspires me to find new ways for people to teach each other. Even if I'm asked to give a lecture on one of my recent books, I always try to provide an opportunity for participants to become the teachers. When they put themselves out there as a role model or subject matter expert, as someone who's a credible source of information, I know and they know that they've got to reach inside a lot deeper than if I just ask them to take part in a simulation. I do that, too, but it's the teaching they do afterward that's the most important part of the experience. That's when you know you've internalized it, made it a part of you. And when you've internalized it, you can externalize it; you can teach it to others.

The richness in this lesson has also led me to realize that master teachers and learners are master storytellers. All we know about each other, we know through the pictures we show and the stories we tell. The rest remains hidden. The more effectively I enable participants to reach inside and reveal something they've learned from their own experiences, the more effectively I teach. And the more capable I am at finding and telling my own story, the more authentically I learn. Learning and teaching, teaching and learning—what a joyous adventure it's been and continues to be!

It seems to me there are only two reasons great teachers know more than their students: One, they've dedicated themselves to learning, and two, they love what they're learning. Come to think of it, maybe that's just one reason.

QUESTIONS

✢ *What is one leadership lesson that you'd most like to learn, and how can you teach it to someone else?*

✢ *As a manager, how might you let your employees teach you?*

✢ *As a parent, how might you let your children teach you?*

✢ *How can you turn your workplace into a classroom where people are always learning and always teaching?*

11 JAMES BELASCO

Dr. James Belasco has led a major computer software and service firm through ten years of phenomenal growth and high margins. He also grew the revenues of a specialty chemical business to the highest margins and market share in its niche. He is author of the bestsellers Teaching the Elephant to Dance *and* Flight of the Buffalo, *and coauthor of the books* Soaring with the Phoenix: Renewing the Vision, Reviving the Spirit and Re-creating the Success of Your Company, *and* Seize Tomorrow, Start Today: Renew Your Vision, Revitalize Your Organization, and Stay Ahead of the Future. *As the founder of San Diego State University's Management Development Center, with previous tenure at SUNY-Buffalo and Cornell, Dr. Belasco has over twenty years' experience opening doorways to new management structures and reinvention techniques.*

The Learner's Point of View

One of my most important learning experiences occurred when I was a doctoral student and teaching assistant for Professor Emil Mesics at Cornell University in the School of Industrial and Labor Relations. In his large class, Professor Mesics gave the two one-hour lectures, and his graduate assistants taught the follow-up small-group discussion sections.

Each week, the three TAs met with Professor Mesics to put together the topics for the discussion sections, and then each of us went off on our own and taught our particular sections. Professor Mesics observed our classes twice each semester and met with us later to give us feedback on our performance.

Now, Professor Mesics was an unusual professor. He didn't have a Ph.D., having come to his professorship as a practitioner, not a researcher. He pioneered the concept and practice of on-the-job training for the Radio Corporation of America (RCA) during World War II and won many accolades and awards for his efforts. His reputation as a practitioner was precisely the attraction for me. I enrolled to earn my doctorate in 1963, fully intending to return to industry after graduation. The chance to learn from a master practitioner motivated me to lobby hard to become Professor Mesics' TA. I was overjoyed to be chosen and vowed I'd do whatever it took to get a great recommendation from him. I knew that doing well on his observation visits was critical to achieving my goal.

Professor Mesics gave me two weeks' notice of his intention to visit my class. While I appreciated the early notice, it immobilized me. I wanted desperately to be a brilliant lecturer with him in the classroom. Yet I'd never taught before, nor had any formal instruction in teaching methodology. Everything I knew about teaching I'd learned either by watching my dad, who was a high school teacher, or by sitting in a classroom for eighteen years—hardly adequate preparation for excellence. My self-doubts and anxiety about my teaching skill kept me awake for most of the two weeks.

In my usual over-prepare crisis mode, I developed an extensive lesson plan. I coached the class on how to behave on that crucial visitation day. I even promised things that I would not want to repeat here to ensure that I'd get the "right" behavior during the critical fifty-minute time period when Emil Mesics sat in my classroom.

On that fateful day, I arrived early at the classroom and wrote my class outline, overhead questions, and key points on the chalkboard. I was pacing the classroom an hour before the first student walked in. The class went better than I ever could have hoped. The students asked good questions. The students answered my questions. The students participated. And my lecture was right on the mark. Afterward Professor Mesics came up to me, shook my hand, and said, "That was a brilliant class. I've taken some notes. Could we talk after the next lecture?" I was on cloud nine when I left the classroom.

After Professor Mesics' next lecture, we went back to his office for our review of his notes, and I was certain I would receive some more praise for the great job I had done. He began, "It was a great class. You are a gifted lecturer. You are energetic and enthusiastic, and that's contagious in your classroom. You engage and involve your students at high levels of discussion. You're a brilliant teacher. Tell me, though, what do you think the students learned?"

His question stopped me cold. I frantically searched for an answer, feeling the sweat begin to break out across my forehead. "Well," I said haltingly, "I had my main points on the board and kept coming back to them. They likely learned them."

Professor Mesics then asked, "How do you know they learned those points?"

I stumbled and stuttered, and finally said, "They answered the questions I put to them. Doesn't that show they learned those points?"

"What is the relationship between the questions you asked and what they really learned? All I heard from their answers was that they knew the answers to your questions, as if the whole exercise had been rehearsed. My question is still the same. What do you think they learned?"

Squirming like a six-year-old boy caught with his hand in the cookie jar, I had to admit, "I don't really know."

Professor Mesics was a kind and gentle man. Sensing my extreme discomfort, he leaned forward and asked softly, "Jim, why do you think I spend fifty minutes with you every week?"

"To learn," I answered meekly.

"Precisely," he said. He then proceeded to dissect my lecture, like a cadaver in the morgue, in terms of my four key points and my questions. At each juncture he asked me what I wanted the students to learn and if I knew whether they had learned it. I couldn't answer a single one of his questions in the affirmative.

Finally he leaned back in his chair and said, "Jim, the most important outcome of that fifty minutes spent in your classroom is not what you do; it's what they leave with. It's not what you teach that's important; it's what they learn that matters most. And the only way you ever know what they learn is to see your lesson plan from their point of view."

Professor Mesics' insight lit my path for a lifetime. I can point to a trillion examples of how seeing it from the learner's perspective made a big difference in my behavior. For example, in every management situation (and all management situations are truly learning situations) I begin by describing the situation from the other players' viewpoints. I then identify how I can best help them be more effective in doing what they need to do.

I've also come to realize the power of another of his messages. Professor Mesics was most proud of his graduates—those people with whom he had worked, who then left to go on to bigger and better things. "Develop successful graduates," Professor Mesics repeatedly told me. They were just words to me when I first heard them thirty-five years ago. Today they are my personal mantra. The graduates of the "Jim Belasco School of Management" are my greatest legacies. For, as Professor Mesics imprinted on my brain, I know that my value as a teacher is measured by the performance of my students. It's not what I do that matters; it's what my students do in life that really counts. I am proud to be one of Emil Mesics' graduates.

QUESTIONS

✝ *How can you best help your graduates succeed?*

✝ *What do you want your students to learn?*

✝ *How will you know if they've learned it?*

12   PAUL HERSEY

Paul Hersey has been a business executive, a professor of management and organizational behavior, a department chairman, a dean, and a university president. He is chairman of the board of the Center for Leadership Studies, the home of Situational Leadership®: a Distinguished Professor of Leadership Studies; Nova S.E. University, and University Professor at Alliant University. He is also a father of six, grandfather of seventeen, and a great grandfather of three.

Standing on the Shoulders of Giants

In my freshman year at the University of Arizona, I decided to major in commercial art. I had always possessed a certain flair for drawing and it seemed like a good choice. I discovered, however, that I had real difficulty doing what other people wanted me to do and so a career in commercial art would not suit me. I learned very quickly that ability is not the only factor for being successful, that you really have to have motivation, commitment, and passion for what you are doing in addition to the skill. At that point, I changed my career plans and earned a degree in management, a brand new field at that time, at Seton Hall University.

A professor under whom I studied saw something in this eager young student and gave me opportunities to capitalize on my passion and my natural instincts for teaching. He let me cover many of his classes when he was not able to be there, and when he left to work at the Industrial Relations Center at the University of Chicago, he offered me a contract as a research associate. In later years, when I was in a position to counsel students as they developed their freshmen schedules, I would encourage them not to declare a major for the first two years of school. Rather, they should take a broad range of classes from professors who were passionate about the subjects they taught, whether it was social sciences, English, or history. My approach was to help them shift from external motivations such as "My father feels strongly that *this* is the field I should go into" or "Accountants (or lawyers, doctors, and so on) make good money" to the internal ones. A great majority of students would change their majors and go on to do something they wanted to do and not something they were pushed into doing.

When I finished my graduate work at the University of Chicago, I worked full time at the Industrial Relations Center for three years and became a project director. I really wanted to be a college professor but felt very strongly that I did not want to contaminate the minds of young people with just my academic credentials; I wanted to have some practical experience to go with the degrees. While perusing *Fortune* magazine, I read that Kaiser Aluminum was going to build the world's largest aluminum-producing plant in a small town in West Virginia. I got on the phone, offered my services to Kaiser, and was hired as the training director. It was an invaluable experience as I was involved in the startup operations as well as training. I spent three years there and was then ready for a new challenge. I interviewed with several companies that today we would call high tech and spent the next four years with Sandia Corporation in Albuquerque, where I was responsible for the technical orientation and management training.

I now had ten years of practical experience, and even though it was a financial hardship, I left the industrial world and got a job as an assistant professor at approximately a quarter of my previous salary. I had made that commitment ten years before, and I felt very good about teaching. The opportunity to enrich a student's academic career and even be a catalyst for change was a special one. Even now, more than forty years later, I am continually hearing from students who share with me that I have changed their lives. That's a very powerful impact to have on someone.

While I was at Kaiser Aluminum in the 1950s, a powerful learning event occurred for me. One evening, well after work hours, I was typing some training material when the industrial relations superintendent came in and saw me typing. He hit the ceiling. He said, "The next time I see you at a typewriter, you will get paid as a secretary. We don't pay you to do that kind of stuff." His comment became a turning point for me as I realized that I should be doing the things I do well and be willing to delegate other tasks to those who did them well. Since then I have applied that lesson to ordinary tasks such as mowing the lawn or hiring someone to fix the plumbing. It comes down to capitalizing on one's strengths.

You can take this a step further by helping people find their own greatness. I think everyone has a spark of greatness that needs to be given the opportunity to burn. One of the hardest lessons we all need to learn is to gain confidence in other people and to turn over responsibility—not too soon, mind you, but we can help others get ready to take on that responsibility.

I enjoyed my career in the academic world immensely, but I was reaching only a small segment of the population, even with a full academic load. I decided that I could influence more people by being in the training business and hiring bright, talented young people to work with me. That was how the Center for Leadership Studies started. Through the Center and other Situational Leadership® training programs, I estimate that we reach several million people a year via textbooks, workshops, and videotapes.

If I were to summarize the way I feel about life, I would quote Sir Isaac Newton, who said, "If I have been able to see further than others, it is because I stood on the shoulders of giants." I had the ability to look farther over the horizon by standing on the shoulders of men like Carl Rogers, Douglas McGregor, and Abraham Maslow, giants in the field. I can only hope that I have had an impact on this younger generation of Blanchards, Goldsmiths, and others. Who could ask for better than that?

In Lewis Carroll's *Alice in Wonderland*, Alice arrives at the intersection of many roads; looking up she sees the Cheshire cat smiling from the tree above. She asks the cat, "Which road should I take?" and he responds, "Where is it you'd like to go?" Alice replies, "I really don't know." The cat responds, "Then take any road."

QUESTION

✢ *It's your life; do you know the direction you want to go? If so, which road will you take?*

13

HOMA BAHRAMI

*Homa Bahrami is an internationally known educator,
advisor, and author who specializes in organizational
flexibility and organizational innovation in knowledge-
based enterprises. She is a researcher, board member, and
executive educator for business and professional organizations worldwide. Bahrami has been the coauthor of two
major textbooks:* Managerial Psychology *(published by
the University of Chicago Press) and* Super-Flexibility for
Knowledge Enterprises *(published by Springer). She is a
Senior Lecturer and a Faculty Director at the Haas
School of Business, University of California Berkeley, is on
the Board of the Haas Center for Teaching Excellence,
and was a research associate at the Graduate School of
Business, Stanford University.*

Nurturing Learning Partnerships

My perspective on learning has been shaped by a succession of
experiences, some of them anchored in my childhood and others rooted
in more recent interactions. These cumulative experiences have gradu-
ally coalesced into my teaching and learning philosophy as an educator,
advisor, and researcher. There was no one transformational event, but
rather a series of personal experiences that have shaped my perspective
as a teacher and a lifelong student.

THREE ESSENTIALS OF EDUCATION

I think of myself as an educator, whether I am wearing the "hat" of professor, board member, mentor, or advisor. My philosophy is based on three building blocks. The first is empathy. I try to understand the uniqueness of each individual and never engage in a standardized "one size fits all" approach. The second building block revolves around energy and enthusiasm, or what may be considered as heightened interest or a sense of passion for the subject. Simply put, I do not enjoy teaching about subjects that I do not care about. I limit my work to subjects that are important to me and that I am curious about. The third block is subject-matter expertise and a willingness to continue to learn.

EMPATHY

The importance of empathy, or trying to see things from the other person's point of view, became evident largely as a result of my childhood and teenage experiences. I am Persian by birth but was raised and educated in England. Growing up in a country and a culture different from the one I was born into affected me greatly. The boarding school I attended brought me in touch with many different cultures; my fellow students came from all over the world. It was like growing up in a small-scale United Nations.

I learned during my teenage years that one culture measures success differently from another. When I was fifteen, I was invited by a close school friend to spend the summer holiday at her family's home in Kenya. I never forget the feeling I had as I walked in a mansion with a large household staff. I realized that the number of servants one had was the measure of one's wealth and status in Africa at that time. In England, I observed that success was often measured by where you went to school, your parents' occupations, and what socioeconomic group you belonged to. Having now lived in the United States for many years, I have observed that Americans are measured by what they do, by how much money they make, and by their tangible accomplishments.

The real insight I gained through my multicultural experiences was how we are all different yet similar. We all value recognition, desire self-esteem, want to improve our circumstances, and value education in one form or another. Yet those common values are implemented in different ways. Empathy gives us a multidimensional lens, an opportunity to appreciate that people from different cultures strive to achieve similar goals but go about implementing them in different ways.

An example of how I apply empathy to my work can be seen in my approach to teaching in different countries. When I teach in Asia, I tend to lecture and focus on conveying core content. In Asian cultures, the teacher is the expert from whom students want to learn and absorb knowledge. This is quite different from the approach I find effective in the United States, where the teacher is more a facilitator. American students want the opportunity to discuss and share their own views. In Europe, I emphasize theory, because there is a lot of interest in tracing the genesis of a particular idea. I try to understand my audience so I can select an approach that would be most effective. My work is always anchored in empathy.

ENERGY AND ENTHUSIASM

The words *energy* and *enthusiasm* capture the second block of my teaching philosophy. Two sets of experiences stand out in my mind. I became aware of their importance as a middle school student in England. The subject of my particular interest was history, which in the hands of many teachers could be very dry. Two history teachers talked about the subjects in a way that was so vivid, so vital and real, it was almost as if I were living the experiences they described.

In one instance, I remember learning about a major battle of World War I. My teacher made me feel the pain of those who suffered and the loss of an entire generation of young men. History became a living drama; I felt like a participant instead of a student in a lecture hall. When teachers have energy and enthusiasm, students experience their passion. It is this passion that keeps demanding audiences interested and involved week after week.

Energy and enthusiasm characterized two mentors who influenced me greatly when I was a postdoctoral fellow at Stanford in the early

1980s. Hal Leavitt, a distinguished professor, showed enthusiasm in the form of curiosity. He always asked piercing questions and was always interested in what I had to say. He probed issues with an almost child-like curiosity that I found engaging. I try to follow his example in my own work today.

Lee Bach, a distinguished economist, demonstrated a compelling interest in, and passion for, his subject matter. I had the opportunity to work with him as a research associate and witnessed his profound interest in searching for multiple answers, trying to unravel different points of view. He was not satisfied with a single answer and would probe deeper and deeper by asking more questions.

I think of myself as a perpetual learner. Whether I'm standing in front of a classroom or coaching an executive, I try to walk away from every session with a new idea, an interesting insight, an illustrative example. I continuously replace my teaching material and upgrade it with new discoveries and insights. Hal Leavitt and Lee Bach inspired me to be a teacher who thirsts for knowledge, is never self-satisfied, and is always open to new possibilities.

EXPERTISE

Expertise involves knowing your own limitations and not pretending to be an expert when you do not have sufficient knowledge. This third block evolved from my work with entrepreneurs in Silicon Valley. I observed that in knowledge-based companies, people have a way of seeing through things rather quickly. A junior software programmer asks her boss a question. The boss gives a vague and rambling answer. The programmer dismisses the boss as someone who does not have the expertise, and the boss instantly loses credibility.

Facilitating executive meetings has helped me understand the importance of subject matter expertise, as well as knowing when to apply that expertise, when to listen to others, and when to admit that you do not have any answers. When executive teams get together to strategize, they dig deeply and examine a topic from every possible angle. A facilitator has to add value at the deepest level. Knowing the latest buzzwords does not equip one with the expertise needed to help demanding clients.

I prepare for a session with the assumption that I will learn from it just as my client will. I know it has been a success if we all come out of the session having created something together. I have little regard for the guru approach. I think of myself as a midwife, helping others give birth to ideas. The guru model is irrelevant today. It has been replaced by peer-to-peer learning, where teachers and students are colleagues in forging learning partnerships.

Feedback is critical for the success of this model. I have found frequent, interim feedback invaluable in teaching my MBA classes. My effectiveness as a teacher is limited if I can only see things from my point of view. If I solicit feedback periodically, I can make midcourse corrections. Seeking feedback is the critical step that synthesizes the three blocks of my philosophy. I need empathy to understand that my students are unique with life experiences solely their own. In asking their opinions, I give them respect and demonstrate that they are valued colleagues in our learning partnership. Finally, I have to demonstrate expertise and enthusiasm for the subject to keep them engaged.

Ultimately, we must look deeply inside ourselves and answer the hard questions: who we really are, what our values and priorities are, and the tradeoffs we are willing to make. You can't teach others unless you know who you are and what makes you tick.

QUESTIONS

✢ *What learning styles best suit you? What makes you tick?*

✢ *What styles have you found that consistently work in teaching others?*

Key Learning Points:
Leading, Learning, and Teaching

It is interesting (and one of the underlying premises of this collection of stories) that the best teachers are those who never stop learning. The difficult issue for most is whether and how to move continually back and forth between teaching and learning. And how does one gain the insight to know when both opportunities present themselves? Parker Palmer in *The Courage to Teach* says, "In every class I teach, my ability to connect with my students, and to connect them with the subject, depends less on the methods I use than on the degree to which I know and trust my selfhood—and am willing to make it available and vulnerable in the service of learning."

After reading the preceding chapters, consider the following questions to check your ability to be an "expert":

✢ *Reflecting on times you have taught, consider what you learned. What knowledge was reinforced? What new knowledge or abilities did you discover?*

✢ *What are the different environments that you utilize to teach others? What opportunities exist in your life now to take advantage of learning by teaching others?*

✢ *What are your stories about significant learning experiences you have had while engaged in teaching others?*

SEEING
YOURSELF AS
OTHERS DO

NATHANIEL BRANDEN

Reach into Yourself to Understand Others

***

JAY CONGER

Lessons on Life from the Goddess of Love

***

CARLOS E. MARIN

Before Lunging Forward, Take a Step Back

14

NATHANIEL BRANDEN

With a Ph.D. in psychology and a background in philoso-
phy, Dr. Branden is a practicing psychotherapist, a busi-
ness consultant, and the author of many books, including
The Six Pillars of Self-Esteem *and* Self-Esteem at
Work. *The latter work deals with his special interest in*
the challenges confronting a business organization in an
information economy.

Reach into Yourself to Understand Others

Anyone who engages in the practice of psychotherapy knows that it is oftentimes as much a learning experience for the therapist as for the client. Nearly forty years ago, I conducted a therapy group in which there was a man, a few years younger than I, with whom I had great difficulty relating. He was passive to a degree I had rarely encountered; he seemed to have a soul I can only describe as "limp."

He showed up at the group meetings regularly and on time, and he answered questions if asked, but he rarely initiated anything. And for the life of me, I could not make contact with that spark every therapist has to count on—that thing within a person that wants to live, that wants to be happy, that wants to do more than simply lie down and surrender to uncontested pain.

On the infrequent occasions when he would ask to work on his problems, nothing we attempted ever seemed to lead anywhere. If we had what I felt was a productive session, by the following week it was as if it had never happened: He evidently had thought about nothing and retained nothing. I came to think of him as passivity incarnate. I thought of him as "the waif of the universe"—wistful, slack-lipped, helpless, and limp. As the weeks and then months passed, I grew more and more frustrated.

It's always been important to me to give every client I work with the experience of total and absolute respect. But one day with this man, I lost it—I exploded in exasperation and spoke as I had never spoken to a client before or ever would again. I said something like: "I need to tell you what I am experiencing right now. I am feeling that I hate the profession I'm in—hate doing this kind of work. I feel totally incompetent and that our sessions are futile. Nothing I know is worth anything when I'm dealing with you."

Sure, I confined myself to "I" statements and avoided "you" statements, but what I said was devastating just the same. That night, telling my wife about the event, I was horrified by what I had done. It went against everything I believed. It was totally out of character. What was the matter with me?

I could not get the incident out of my mind, and a few days later at dinner with another couple, both of whom were therapists, I described what had happened and my mystified shock at my behavior. The man, Hal Stone, said to me, "May I offer a psychological interpretation?" Of course, I invited him to proceed.

"I don't think," he said, "you have any trouble recognizing and owning most of your emotions: fear, anger, lust, or whatever. But I suspect there is one feeling you would never permit yourself and therefore would not recognize when it occurred. And yet all of us, simply by virtue of being human, would have to have that feeling once in a while. I'm talking about the feeling of passive helplessness. I suspect that the part of you that would experience such a feeling is disowned, split off from the rest of you, so that you're oblivious to it. And then—in the person of this client—fate sends you a caricature of this disowned piece of yourself. And I suspect that's why you reacted as you did."

Instantly I felt that what he was saying was true.

The next week with the group, I told everyone about what had been revealed to me. I apologized to my client. I said, "If I could not recognize and accept the part of me that sometimes feels as you do, if that part was denied and disowned by me, there is no way I would be able to work with you productively."

My client seemed to come to life in front of my eyes. He felt understood. He felt accepted. After that, therapy took off and we began to make progress. What I learned from this experience was that whatever I deny and disown within myself becomes a limitation on my effectiveness in working with others.

Today, in addition to practicing psychotherapy, I do corporate consulting, and the same principle is operative in that context. If, for example, I am working with a CEO or another executive who is resisting necessary change, I know that if I can make contact with the part of myself that sometimes resists necessary change, I will be more effective. If I am coaching a brilliant engineer who has difficulty working as a member of a team, I know that if I can connect with the part of myself that is attached to being the Lone Ranger, I will be more effective. If I am working with a manager who feels much more comfortable managing technology than managing people, I know that if I can connect with the part of me that can get impatient when people do not instantly grasp what I want them to grasp—and who sometimes hates to be bothered with "psychology"—I will be more effective.

I will be more effective because—being more empathetic—I will cause the person to feel psychologically visible. Feeling understood, he or she will be more open to new learnings and more willing to experiment with new ways of operating.

Self-awareness is the foundation of emotional intelligence and interpersonal competence.

QUESTIONS

✢   *Do you know someone who irritates/frustrates/confounds you? What is it about this person that causes you to react as you do?*

✢   *Can you empathize with this person? Can you see something of yourself in this person, past or present?*

✢   *Think of some strategies that you use (consciously or unconsciously) to keep from being your "limp" self. Would any of these strategies help this person?*

15 JAY CONGER

*Jay Conger is a professor of organizational behavior at the
London Business School and senior research scientist at the
University of Southern California. The author of more
than sixty articles and eight books, he researches leadership,
organizational change, boards of directors, and the training and development of managers and executives. His
most recent books include* Winning 'Em Over: A New
Model for Management in the Age of Persuasion, The
Leader's Change Handbook, *and* Charismatic Leadership in Organizations. *One of Conger's greatest passions
is teaching. He has received numerous teaching awards
and was selected by* BusinessWeek *as the best business
school professor to teach leadership to executives. As a
former archaeologist, he enjoys living life fully and always
with a sense of adventure.*

Lessons on Life from the Goddess of Love

This is the story of the summer I spent in Aphrodisias, an ancient Turkish city named for the goddess of love. What I learned that
summer about life, about the passage of time, and about living life well
changed me profoundly.

During that summer, I gained a deep appreciation for the speck
of time each of our lives represents. I learned that the time we have

is precious. The evidence of mortality of the wealthy, powerful, and famous—people whose names are long lost—was a humbling reminder that quests to leave a legacy are almost always a fantasy. My experiences instilled in me a deep belief that we have to find ways to do what is intrinsically rewarding every day of our lives. If we don't, we will waste the experience and lose the precious opportunity of our own short moment here.

I was nineteen that summer and had just finished my sophomore year. An anthropology major, I was lucky to have landed a job with the National Geographic Society. I would be joining a team of archaeologists at Aphrodisias, a remote site in southwestern Turkey, hours away from the nearest city.

This was extremely good fortune, as Aphrodisias was one of the most important cities of ancient times. As a Greek and Roman city, it had enjoyed a span of several hundred years in which it was one of the most important centers for art and architecture. People in every Roman city wanted to have works from Aphrodisias, because its sculpting schools were renowned throughout the region. Unlike most Roman sculptors, who were famous for copying Greek works, Aphrodisians were renowned for their originality.

The city was situated in a valley between two mountain ranges. Its earliest inhabitants were prehistoric peoples who had settled on a very large hill in the center of the valley. Strategically it was a great location because the land was fertile, there was water, and from the hill, approaching enemies could be seen from either direction. Eventually the little town grew into a Greek city and then a Roman city of several hundred thousand people.

My job for the summer was to work with ninety Turkish workmen to unearth the theater of Aphrodisias. The Frenchman who had first discovered it in the 1800s only guessed at the theater when he found fragments of marble seats on the top of that large hill. While prehistoric peoples had built villages there, the Romans saw the hillside as a natural amphitheater and built into it seats rising up the hillside, using the hill as the support system. It had been a huge theater, holding about 4,000 people. But over the millennia, earthquakes and time had filled in the theater, and the upper portions had collapsed and tumbled down into the lower portions. By the Middle Ages, little evidence of it remained. Our job was to unearth the theater, remove the fill, and restore it to its original form.

My crew of workmen came from a village a kilometer away. They walked out to the dig each morning and returned to their village at the end of the day. While the men were friendly, they were a rough-and-tumble crowd who could grow violent over a minor disagreement—the kind of people I had been isolated from as a student. There were other cultural challenges as well. For instance, they spoke only Turkish and, at the outset, I spoke none. Yet I was to be their crew boss. I learned quickly.

Every day our dig took us further back in time. We could see that as the ancient city declined in importance, and ultimately when the Romans left, the grandeur disappeared. The city evolved into a series of small Byzantine villages and then a series of Islamic villages. Parts of these villages were built inside the amphitheater because it was naturally protected. We had to unearth layer after layer of the villages that had risen inside this amphitheater to ultimately expose the original building.

While digging, I'd find coins that had been hidden in the ancient village walls and everyday pottery that had been broken and forgotten. I'd find tools and hordes of seemingly precious possessions that people had hidden away so they wouldn't be stolen. What I began to see most clearly was the passing of time and people. Over the course of the summer, we dug through two thousand years. We were going down almost fifty years each day—the span of a long lifetime in those ancient days. The evidence of lives spent was powerful and moving.

When the workmen returned to their village at the end of each day, our small band of archaeologists had the whole ancient city to ourselves. In the evenings I would always go for a walk in the ruins. There's something magical about the night in Turkey. At dusk, the sky turns a brilliant, rich, pink-orange color, and as the night wears on, the Milky Way extends from horizon to horizon. I was swept away by this breathtaking, natural beauty that highlighted a foreground of ancient temples, marble walkways, and beautiful sculptures. It was as if we had a museum all to ourselves for two and a half months—a museum without a roof, a museum the size of a city that once held 300,000 people.

There was a powerful sense of mystery to the place. The site itself was spectacular, with several beautiful temples, marble streets, storefronts, homes, and palaces. There was an enormous stadium that had held about 20,000 people. I would wander alone at night among these fabulous ruins, and as I walked, the wind would whip through the stadium, and I could hear 20,000 Romans cheer their favorite team.

The poignant realization hit me early on that one day a thousand years from now some young archaeologist would be unearthing my period of time where I had lived. I would be much like the pile of stones and rubble that made up one of the little village houses.

I learned another lesson there, too. The theater, as well as many of the monuments, had been built by very wealthy and powerful individuals whose names were carved on the imposing marble structures. One distinguished person had given this building to the city and another had given that one. At the time, these were the most powerful individuals in the city and, often, powerful citizens of Rome. Yet nobody knows any of them today. They are simply names on a wall. And they had been the most accomplished citizens of their time. The lesson was that no one endures forever. I too shall pass, and whatever fame I might have is brief. Learning this was profoundly humbling.

Shelley wrote of Ozymandias—an Egyptian pharaoh whose sculpted head rested in the sand: "My name is Ozymandias, king of kings: Look on my works, ye mighty, and despair!" One sees simply the broken head of the pharaoh; his greatness has vanished.

I began to see firsthand that the impact of powerful people has a limited legacy, despite the fact that they may live on in our public works or art or books. We live on through our children and grandchildren, but that's about it. The lesson is to live well for today, for yourself and for your family. Do not simply hope you will live for what you leave behind.

During this time, I felt a sense of paradox because of the grandeur and mystery of life that was around me. When I wandered through the ancient towns that people once lived and thrived in, I felt connected with a higher power—something indeed eternal. I felt there must be a God out there because I sensed the power of the natural beauty and the human beauty blended together.

Of course, Aphrodite is the goddess of love. And really, what all of this is about—in a strange way—is love. If you love life and you love yourself and you love the people you're with, you have an obligation to develop them and yourself. And if you love yourself, you will always do things for your betterment rather than things that harm you.

Like the Turkish sunsets, that summer at Aphrodisias has colored every day of my life, in that I keenly feel how fleeting and precious time is. It became extremely important for me to discover my gifts and realize my potential early on so I could make my own short time on this planet truly count.

The other lesson powerfully reinforced by the experience of Aphrodisias was the certain knowledge that my name won't really live on—that to spend one's life trying to build a name that will live on is an illusion. Doing what is intrinsically rewarding for me and for the people with whom I live and work is really what is valuable—building a living daily legacy rather than the illusion of a permanent, immortal legacy.

QUESTIONS

☦ *Knowing that my legacy is not eternal, how shall I live today?*

☦ *What can you do in your life today that is intrinsically rewarding for you and people with whom you live and work?*

☦ *How can you be a better teacher and developer of others today?*

16 CARLOS E. MARIN

Carlos Marin is a highly experienced International Executive Coach and Leadership Development Consultant with twenty-five years of experience assisting hundreds of leaders and their organizations throughout the world. He is the former vice president of the Human Development Training Institute in San Diego and Founder, Dean, and Chancellor of the National University campus in San Jose, Costa Rica. An experienced international consultant and leadership development educator, Marin has worked with such companies as American Express Companies, the Coca-Cola Company, Merck Sharp & Dhome, Siemens, Unilever, Sempra Energy, and Wells Fargo. He has been a lifelong student and practitioner of martial arts, specifically t'ai chi ch'uan, tae kwon do, aikido, and karate do.

Before Lunging Forward, Take a Step Back

Try to recall a time when something just came together in your mind, when you had a wonderful "aha!" experience, when you "got it." Recall that effortless, powerful feeling that comes out of experiencing harmony between the intellectual, the emotional, and the physical parts of us.

I have spent much of my life practicing martial arts and experiencing important learning breakthroughs from the teachings of these disciplines. As a young teacher of high school students, I became curious about the fact that some students would often credit me with the ability to make things easy for them to understand. Later in my career, people would come to me after I had taught a class or facilitated a group and express how I had helped them "connect" with the content of the presentation. Often they would relate how they had "experienced" the material. As I reflected on what I was doing, I related my teaching to my experiences in martial arts.

I came into martial arts with the desire to learn about self-defense. As a kid, I had several episodes and encounters in which my ability to take care of myself was questionable. I was twelve years old when, encouraged by my father, I went to watch a judo class. I found the experience so interesting that I asked my folks to let me sign up for lessons. I was fortunate to start with a teacher (sensei) who was patient and demanding at the same time. Over time, he encouraged me to develop the discipline to train consistently and to experience going beyond the self-imposed limits of what I thought I could do. The more I practiced, the more confident I became, learning to be quieter inside and more aware of my surroundings.

This process began to influence the way I approached my social world. In judo class we worked on "sensing" the movement and breathing of others. I would ask for explanations of how to do this, and Sensei's response was, "Let your body do it. Don't think—just do it." How could I learn something I did not understand? "Practice, practice," he insisted; and practice I would. This training in perception was helping me develop the ability to focus, to "tune in," and to sense signals from people.

My formal educational process emphasized the importance of rationality, analysis, and conceptual understanding. I was taught to approach challenges with an analytical mind-set, to separate the parts of a problem in order to come to a solution.

As I continued my learning journey in the martial arts disciplines, I had wonderful teachers in the various disciplines. Eventually I had the fortune of meeting Al Chung Liang Huang, a gifted Tai Chi teacher, who once said to me, "*Soften your eyes and you will see more.*" I was in the "trying hard to see" mode, attempting to make sense of a section of the tai chi "form" we were doing. As I practiced his suggestion, I became aware of the tension in my eyes; I began feeling the muscles of my eyes relaxing and my visual field expanding. This process is equivalent to changing lenses, where patterns of connections and dynamic interrelationships are highlighted.

In the practice of a tai chi form called "The Five Elements," the first movement is a deliberate step backward accompanied by an opening gesture of the arms as extension of your eyes. This is not just a physical gesture; it is a psychological one. It is a "clearing" movement aimed at emptying one's perspective to invite the surrounding realities to fill your senses. The message is simple: before you lunge forward, take a step back, as a wider field may present you with more options.

In my work, I often see people craning their heads forward, frowning, squinting their eyes, struggling to understand, to analyze, and to unearth the logic in what they perceive to be happening. When they walk, it seems as if their heads are moving heavily ahead of the rest of their bodies. I see and feel their frustration, their tension. I can hear the stress in their voices, and I invite them to take a deep breath, to sit back and relax and be "present" for a moment, then to sense what is happening as opposed to thinking about it. I may also suggest that they witness their problem or challenge from this new place—a place that requires a "softer," but by no means weaker, attitude.

Helping people make a transition to a more relaxed, attentive presence enables them to see in renewed ways. Over the years, I have played with this process, and it has become an important tool in my professional practice. It helps people learn more about themselves and others.

First, clear your inner space by suspending your assumptions. Take a step back, and soften your eyes. Now see with "new eyes" that can take you on a learning journey of your own, where you are a more refined instrument of perception. With practice, your renewed and softer eyes may help you find the experience that leads you to that "aha" feeling or that harmonious "I got it" sensation.

QUESTIONS

‡   *Can you let your expert eyes relax so that you may see what your expertise may be covering up?*

‡   *Is stress or tension stopping you from seeing solutions?*

‡   *How can you apply this process of softening your perception to help yourself and others see with new eyes?*

Key Learning Points:
Seeing Yourself as Others Do

When we are able to step back, watch what is occurring around us, and see ourselves from the perspectives of others, we are using our "third eye." Stepping back enables us to see things in a broader view. Often we are so caught up with the politics and emotions of what is happening in our lives that we are unable to relax and gain this larger view, but when we slow down and see things from another perspective, great clarity and learning can occur.

After reading the preceding questions, consider the following questions related to this "third eye" learning experience:

✢ *When do you pause to reflect on your life and the factors that contribute to current events and situations?*

✢ *Describe a scenario in which your perspective changed when you stepped back.*

✢ *Can you teach others to step back in order to experience an objective perspective? How?*

✢ *In the heat of the moment it can be difficult to step outside the situation and see things from a broad perspective. How do you remind yourself to breathe and take a look around before proceeding?*

DEVELOPING
SELF-KNOWLEDGE

DAVE ULRICH

An Allegory for Learning ... and Meaning

SPENCER JOHNSON

Integrity or out of Tegrity?

ELIZABETH PINCHOT

Sometimes It Takes an Elbow in the Ribs

NANCY J. ADLER

Recognizing Leadership, Trusting Life

17

DAVE ULRICH

Dave Ulrich, a professor at the Ross School of Business at the University of Michigan and partner at the RBL group (www.rbl.net), has received numerous recognitions and awards from BusinessWeek, Forbes, HR Magazine, Fast Company, and Executive Excellence. He is the author of twenty-two books on human resources, leadership, culture, and talent. His work focuses on how internal organization actions (HR, leadership, culture) deliver value to employees inside the company and customers, investors, and communities outside.

An Allegory for Learning . . . and Meaning

ACT 1:

I was twenty-five years old and had been married four years. We had a young child and another on the way. We had just moved to Los Angeles, where I had started a doctorate program and was trying to eke out a living. And I decided to do something bizarre. In a casual conversation with my father, who was nearing fifty, I asked if he ever got bored (he did) and if he ever wanted to do something out of the ordinary (he did).

In mid-March, in an offhand way, I suggested we ride our bikes from Seattle to Los Angeles in mid-June. On the map it looked downhill.

Both of us were casual cyclists at best and could be described by those being gracious as "heavy" or "robust." My bike cost $99 and had a name sticker taped over the original manufacturer's name. My dad's bike was not much better. Neither of us had been on much more than weekend rides, but, after getting approval from our spouses (with more faith than confidence), we trained for three months and set off on the adventure.

It was a wild ride to say the least. We carried all our gear and food. We did not have great maps to highlight the biker-friendly roads, but we started at the crack of dawn every morning and rode until we were too tired to ride anymore. We did not use fancy biking gear. We experienced bike riding on dirt roads when we got lost; sleeping on picnic tables when we could not find a city nearby and in church basements when we found a city; almost being run off the road by logging trucks when we were on roads with no shoulders; and the joys of broken brakes, flat tires, and replaced spokes. We also received countless honks, signs, and gestures from motorists. But we made it all the way to Santa Monica. After twenty-one days, we completed the 1,400-mile journey.

ACT 2:

Now, almost thirty years later, when my daughter was going through her post-Ph.D. and life blues, she said, "Dad, let's do something bizarre together." And we opted for a bike ride. Not being as adventuresome as my father and I, we rode from Oregon to San Francisco, a more modest ride. We had better bikes and stayed in nicer hotels. But we had the same sore neck, legs, and other body parts. We also had another daughter who drove the supply car and spent time with us in the morning and evening discussions.

But even more, we had some of the same bonding. Little can replace the casual conversations among family while biking by the peaceful ocean, grazing cattle, and fields of green. Physical exercise helps us relieve stress. Social connection creates enduring legacy.

Recently my father passed away. I honor his memory and continue his legacy. My daughters and I may do another bike ride this summer. We continue to be close and supportive of each other in our good times and bad. The physical exercise becomes an excuse for personal connection.

These experiences have become an allegory for many challenges I have faced and lessons I have learned in my last thirty years as professor, researcher, and consultant.

First, I learned about the enduring challenge of balance. My father and I decided to take off in the middle of my doctorate program and while I was struggling to make money. My daughters are both busy: one a professor, the other a psychologist. We find that we like each other and spending time together is renewing and refreshing. As we age, we differ in social and political opinions, but are bonded by shared experiences. Balance of work, family, and personal life has continued to be one of the major challenges of my life. I constantly recalibrate how I am doing in meeting the multiple demands I place on myself. With a granddaughter, I find that family time is ever more sacred. Workshops come and go and professional colleagues are delightful, but family endures.

Second, I learned to appreciate risks. This entire venture was risky. In both cases, we did not train well. We were far from seasoned bikers. We learned to improve equipment and map the route, but mostly we fixed a date, met, then started to ride south.

Understanding risk has been enormously helpful throughout my career. I thought that after thirty years, I would "have it," but frequently I still find myself in meetings with senior managers from large, complex, global firms who are struggling with very difficult issues. After they share their challenges, they often look to me for ideas. At times I wonder, "What in the world am I doing here? I don't have a clue how to deal with this problem." Then I take the risk, become engaged, and muddle through, generally finding that by asking questions, communicating openly to spark dialogue, and continually reframing, I turn risk into results. It was on the bike trips that I learned to face risk and move forward. This has served me well.

Third, I learned about myself. I discovered that I like to achieve. It felt good to clock the miles, to set daily goals and meet them, and to accomplish the overall task. But I also learned that my achievement is less about beating someone else and more about pushing myself to do more. My dad and I, then my daughter and I, found that we worked to support each other on the hills and help each other when down. It was nice to have a friend.

Fourth, I learned about failure. Numerous times on the trip, I felt ready to quit. When my spokes started to snap, when I had the third flat tire, when a logging truck nearly ran me off the road, when my rear end hurt so much I could hardly stand it, I nearly stopped the abuse and said "Enough." But we kept going, and my tolerance for failure and discouragement grew.

This tolerance for failure has served me well. I could cover my walls with rejection letters for manuscripts I felt were more thoughtful and well researched than reviewers did. I have had numerous clients who weren't affected by my ideas the way I thought they would be. I have learned that when things go wrong, I simply need to go forward, learning from the past, but not being bound by it. It still hurts to fail, but moving forward is a useful response.

Finally, I learned about what matters most. By biking together with my father and children, I came to appreciate family in marvelous ways. For these biking oasis days, our family was our life. My father's legacy lives on as I try to pass on to our children a sense of family community. My father spent much of his life in service to others. After he retired at 55, he spent three to four hours, four days a week, doing a "bread run" where he would pick up leftover bread and other items from grocery stores and deliver them to shelters and food banks throughout his city. He was the consummate volunteer who sought to give back to his community and family. I need to remember these lessons and pass this legacy to our children and grandchildren.

In my work, I have found that relationships matter more than projects. I find myself seeking and nurturing relationships of trust with clients. I find that many professional colleagues have become friends. It is a joy and a delight to share both personal and professional experiences with my clients and colleagues.

Recently, Wendy Ultrich and I have studied and published on meaning at work (*The Why of Work*). In these publications, we suggest that when employees find meaning in their work setting, they are more productive and their customers, investors, and communities benefit. Meaning matters. My experiences with my father and children have defined the value of meaning and a critical source to finding it.

QUESTIONS

✣ *How often do we do things that are out of the ordinary?*

✣ *How well do we learn from experiences outside of work that can translate to what happens at work?*

✣ *How do we find meaning in the routines of work and life?*

18 SPENCER JOHNSON

Spencer Johnson, M.D., is an internationally respected thought leader, speaker, and author whose insights have helped millions of people discover simple truths they can use to have healthier lives with more success and less stress. He is author and coauthor of the renowned bestselling books Who Moved My Cheese? *and* The One Minute Manager® *(with Kenneth Blanchard). Other bestsellers include* The Precious Present, Yes or No, ValueTales®, *and five books in the* One Minute® *series:* The One Minute Sales Person, The One Minute Mother, The One Minute Father, The One Minute Teacher, *and* The One Minute for Yourself. *Johnson's books have been featured on CNN, the* Today Show, *and* Larry King Live, *and in* Time Magazine, BusinessWeek, The New York Times, The Wall Street Journal, USA Today, Associated Press, *and United Press International.*

Integrity or out of Tegrity?

My learning journey began in deep pain, but the lessons I learned led me to a wonderful place, a place I gratefully enjoy today. There was a time, about twenty years ago, when, after I had enjoyed some success, things began to go wrong. It was like the confluence of a river—

everything bad came at once (for which I am now grateful; the pain was sufficient to force me to go through it).

Several projects were faltering and I was under financial stress. My life was out of balance. I was going through a divorce. At one level my life had been working, but at much deeper and more important levels it was not working at all. The worst part of it was that it came as a surprise to me. I thought that everything was all right. I thought I was as honest as most people are, but I had been kidding myself.

I went off by myself to take a long, hard look at the life I'd been living. I went to an isolated area where there was no television or radio to distract me. I spent a lot of time walking empty beaches, sort of blank-minded. I just didn't know what had gone wrong with my life. I began to look at when my life had worked and when it hadn't. I spent time alone, day after day, walking or sitting and staring at the water, reflecting on what had happened.

I knew that I wanted to change, but I didn't know what was wrong or how to change. I certainly had a desire to stop the pain, although the pain was becoming a great teacher. It helped me decide that I couldn't continue to live the way I had been living.

I took a panoramic look at my life and saw it as a series of events. After a lot of time being quiet, being still, I began to see some patterns emerge. When I looked back on the areas of my life that worked, I noticed a certain pattern, and when I looked at the areas that didn't work, I saw the opposite pattern. By looking at what worked and what didn't work, I came to the realization that when I was aware of the truth and I lived it, my life went very well. But when I either didn't see the truth or wanted to ignore the truth and proceeded in spite of it, my life didn't work very well. Eventually there were painful consequences. Once I saw the cause of my pain, I began the journey of learning my lesson.

I became intrigued with the challenge of looking for and living the truth—particularly the obvious truth that I wasn't able to see. When I saw it, it became embarrassingly simple. How could I have missed it for so many years? Looking for the truth became my cornerstone. What I learned was that I had the ability to kid myself, to tell myself something that I believed was true but that was never true. My challenge was to start telling myself the truth as often as I could.

I use the word *integrity* to mean telling myself the truth, and the word *honesty* to mean telling others the truth. Once you have integrity, it's fairly easy to have honesty. For me the challenging part was to develop a sense of integrity—which is what you do when no one is watching. I had found out the hard way that getting "out of tegrity"—a state where you lie to yourself, are unaware of it, and believe what you tell yourself—leads to some very serious pain.

Once we go "out of tegrity" we don't see the problems that are coming, problems that we have created. If we can convince ourselves of something that isn't true, we can be pretty persuasive in convincing others, and if we go down a road at the end of which is a lie, everyone involved will experience pain sooner or later. When I look around the world, it seems to me that the source of all pain is a lack of the truth. So, considering the fact that I don't want to spend a lot more time in pain, whether it's financial, physical, or emotional pain, it's important to me to stay "in tegrity," to do all I can to see reality and tell myself the real truth.

Something else I eventually learned from my experience—when the pain subsided—is not to be too hard on myself, to lighten up and have some fun, to enjoy myself even when I realize I have been wrong and have a lot to learn. Now I ask myself, "Have I kept a sense of humor?" I have found that the balance between truth and humor is very nurturing, and ironically, it's very productive. The interesting thing about humor is that humor isn't concerned with productivity. It's just interested in enjoying the moment.

Of the books I have written, my favorite one is *The Precious Present,* because it is about enjoying the moment. That book practically wrote itself very shortly after the time I was on that remote island. I wrote the first half of it in a couple of hours on cocktail napkins while returning on a boat from Catalina. And I wrote the second half a week later one day on my patio. Because it took only two days to write, I was clear that, in a sense, I didn't write the book. It just came through me, effortlessly.

I knew I was getting in touch with the truth, because there was not much ego and more ease.

I have learned that when we are in harmony with reality, things happen very easily. It really doesn't take much effort. It's when we're out of tegrity that we have to stop and say, "Wait a minute. Something's wrong here; I'm working too hard at this."

I have come to ask myself, "Can you feel yourself *feel?*" Up until those long days spent walking the beaches, I had done too many things in my life based on thinking rather than feeling. I had read; I had analyzed; I had thought. I was intellectually educated (Harvard, the Mayo Clinic, and the Royal College of Surgeons) to respect the complicated and discard the simple. I came to realize that what is true for me is pretty much the opposite of what I was taught. I discovered that the simple is much more powerful. Not the simplistic—simplistic is less than what we need. But the simple is all we need and nothing more. And I have never found a great practical truth in my life that wasn't so simple that it was almost embarrassing when I finally saw it.

Another lesson I learned from my painful experience is that our emotions and our egos and our beliefs are not very important. When we laugh we tend to confirm this. Once we get all of that out of the way, we can have a lot of fun being very productive, because the process is not centered on us; we've gotten out of the way. This is a good way to live and a lot more enjoyable for ourselves and for the people around us.

In former days I tried to make things happen. When I realized I needed to let go, to trust in reality and let things happen, everything improved.

The result of living in tegrity for me is that life has gotten dramatically better. I am now joyfully remarried to a wonderful woman, one with great integrity. I have two sons and our family has a wonderful life. So for me this issue of being in tegrity is very, very practical.

I must acknowledge, of course, that I still fall out of tegrity. There are times when I am not aware and not clear. I still make dumb mistakes, but I hope they are fewer each year. I am more and more aware of the need to stay in touch with reality, to tell myself and others the truth—and enjoy it!

QUESTIONS

✢ *Am I telling myself the truth, or am I kidding myself?*

✢ *Integrity or out of tegrity? Which is more enjoyable?*

19 ELIZABETH PINCHOT

Elizabeth Pinchot has been a social entrepreneur for forty years, as well as a consultant and author. In this decade she cofounded the Bainbridge Graduate Institute (BGI) and still works with its innovative MBA programs in sustainable and socially responsible business. Prior to BGI, as president of Pinchot & Company, she coached and trained senior executives in organizations as diverse as the U.S. Forest Service, the Canadian National Railroad, and the New York Stock Exchange. Pinchot also cofounded and ran several small businesses and academic programs, as well as practiced biodynamic farming. She is the coauthor, with Gifford Pinchot, of The Intelligent Organization, *and a Ph.D. student in participative action research at Saybrook University.*

Sometimes It Takes an Elbow in the Ribs

 She sat down next to me in the front row of an auditorium where E. F. Schumacher, who had just become prominent for his book *Small Is Beautiful*, was about to speak. In minutes she had fallen asleep. Margaret, a small, round woman in this last year of her life, was dressed in a navy blue cloak that enveloped her body, so that as she slept in the chair only the short gray hair on top of her head suggested a human sat there.

I knew I was sitting next to Margaret Mead, who had cofounded the discussion group I was attending in Westchester in the mid-1970s, but I had never met her. I had only had her pointed out to me from the other side of the room. Her close presence excited me at first, but after a while my attention was fixed on Schumacher, who was speaking strong words with a demeanor of gentle and humorous wisdom. He was making sense, confirming the importance of my experience in small business and biodynamic farming. During the question-and-answer period with Schumacher, Margaret continued to sleep, but I began to get agitated by the stupidity of a debunking question asked by an elegant woman in Gucci jeans and high-heeled boots. She was saying that ecological agriculture and the localization movement was unworkable and laughably naïve. She was acting like an authority, the harsh voice of reason. I wanted to speak up to her but didn't dare. You have to picture me—I was in my fifth year of residence on an experimental ecological farm and looked the part, with clothes from India, not Italy, and muscles. We were in the Tarrytown Conference Center, housed in the elegant Mary Biddle Duke Estate overlooking the Hudson River. I felt out of place with this crowd of real grown-ups. I couldn't talk in front of strangers.

As Margaret slept on, the woman argued on with Schumacher, and I must have finally gotten angry enough to mutter something hostile under my breath. From the dark-cloaked lump sleeping next to me an elbow shot out into my ribs, hitting hard, and Margaret Mead hissed in my ear:

"Stand up and say your piece."

I did, as best I could, and it made a difference. I had no choice but to make myself heard. I like to remember that elbow in my ribs. I still need it.

QUESTIONS

✢ *What do you care about enough that can get you to say your piece, even if it might be uncomfortable?*

✢   *What do you want to develop in yourself so you can speak your passions?*

✢   *How can you make yourself really heard by those who are unlike you?*

✢   *What might be serving as an elbow in your ribs for speaking strong truths that the world needs to hear?*

20 NANCY J. ADLER

Nancy Adler, Ph.D., is the S. Bronfman Chair in Management at the Desautels Faculty of Management, McGill University, in Montreal, Canada. She conducts research and consults on global strategy, leadership, and cross-cultural management. Adler is the author of more than one hundred articles and has written and edited eight books. She has also produced the films A Portable Life *and* Reinventing Our Legacy. *She has consulted for private corporations and government organizations on projects in Africa, Asia, Europe, North and South America, and the Middle East. Adler has received numerous awards, including Canada's top university teaching award, ASTD's international leadership award, and Sage's management research award. She has been inducted into the Royal Society of Canada and the Fellows of both the Academy of Management and the Academy of International Business. Adler is also a visual artist and has been an artist in residence at The Banff Centre. Her most recent exhibition was "Reality in Translation: Going Beyond the Dehydrated Language of Management." She can be reached at (514) 398-4031 or via e-mail at* nancy.adler@mcgill.ca.

Recognizing Leadership, Trusting Life

Call it serendipity, destiny, or anything else you choose, but a wonderful learning experience happened because a colleague walked into my office one afternoon with a newspaper article that turned out to have an enormous impact on me.

The story is this: I was invited to give the opening keynote address at the Salzburg Seminar's worldwide conference on global leadership. This conference was of particular interest to me because, for the first time in the fifty-year history of the Salzburg Seminar, the focus was to be on women who were global leaders. Anyone who knows me even vaguely knows I am very interested in global leadership and in women leaders from around the world. Initially, however, due to other commitments, I didn't give the conference organizers a definite yes, because I wasn't sure I would have enough time to prepare the type of speech that I most wanted to give.

Not long after I received the invitation, I was working in my Montreal office when a colleague walked in and said, "Nancy, my mom, who is a business reporter for the *Chicago Tribune*, just sent me this article about Charity Ngilu, the first woman ever to run for president of Kenya. She thought you'd be interested in it." As I began reading the story, I was amazed. If I had combined all my research on the forty-seven women who had served as president or prime minister of their respective countries (the number is now eighty-nine) and had tried to write a definitive case study on women leaders, highlighting the courage and drive it takes to become a country's number-one leader, I couldn't have invented a story more compelling than Charity's.

As another colleague said later, it was *b'shert*, or destined. My own upbringing, however, had taught me not to trust in such coincidences. Why? The reason is simple. My mother came from Vienna and left Europe after Hitler marched in. Her family maintained the attitude that you make the important things happen in your life that are positive; they don't just happen to you.

For me, the very concept of synchronicity—of good things happening by coincidence—hadn't even occurred to me until the previous summer, and then only because of the persistent prodding of an artist friend of mine. She had challenged me to notice three positive things that happened to me each day for a week. The good news is that after a few days I began noticing the positive coincidences that were constantly arriving in my life. The bad news is that it had still never occurred to me that positive coincidences—or synchronicity—had anything to do with my professional life.

By the time I finished reading the *Chicago Tribune* article, the speech I wanted to write flowed easily from my fingertips onto my computer screen. The process was nothing like my typical style of writing and rewriting my carefully crafted and well-researched speeches. Rather, the speech seemed to just arrive. It was Charity Ngilu's story, but in my voice, surrounded by the voices of all the other women who have succeeded in leading their countries. Only after the speech had arrived did I spend a few days checking the facts behind Charity's story. After all, once a professor, always a professor.

I flew to Austria for the opening of the Salzburg Seminar. That evening, when I walked to the podium to deliver my keynote address, the words flowed from my mouth, much like they had flowed from my fingertips a few weeks earlier as I wrote the speech.* Even though I give many speeches, I normally get slightly nervous when I deliver a major address to a large international audience, but not this time. I was strangely calm. I didn't even look at my notes.

As I finished the speech, a wonderful Ghanaian woman, a member of Parliament, stood up and told the audience that Charity was her friend and that my speech was very important. Suddenly, Charity became even more alive for me; it was as if she were there in the room.

The next morning, a member of Uganda's Parliament (who had not been able to attend the opening session of the conference the evening before) introduced herself, apologized for having missed my speech,

---

*Adler's Salzburg Seminar keynote address is published as "Did You Hear? Global Leadership in Charity's World." *Journal of Management Inquiry*, 1998, 7(2), pp. 135–143.

and told me that she had spent the previous evening having dinner with Charity Ngilu. She carefully explained to me that the only thing the world community can do to help leaders like Charity is give them global visibility. Global visibility is important because it makes it much more difficult for anyone to silence or harm people such as Charity who are trying to make a difference in the world. As the Ugandan member of Parliament explained, global visibility would help Charity maintain her courage. She repeated what the Ghanaian woman had said the evening before: "Nancy, your speech is very important. Your speech gives Charity visibility, global visibility." Visibility reduces the possibility that courage will be extinguished.

The entire experience had somehow become larger than life. Although people often compliment me on being a good speaker, this time it was as if I had become a conduit through which Charity's story and, what is more important, its meaning, had been delivered. Yes, I had recognized the story and its importance, but I had not created the story—I had merely retold it.

The story isn't about me, it's about Charity Ngilu. But it really isn't about Charity, either. It is about having the courage to make a difference in the world; it is about having the courage to speak out.

Trusting my instincts and letting my intuitive side run the show, allowing myself to become a conduit for the story rather than its scholarly creator, was new to me. I have confidence in my academic and consulting experience. I have studied, learned, taught, and contributed to students, managers, executives, and organizations, but this other way of creating and contributing, this intuitive level, was something special. Serendipitous? Synchronous? I am not saying that I completely understand it, but I am now much more open to its possibilities.

QUESTIONS

✢ *How do we recognize wisdom that is bigger than our personal experience?*

✢ *How do we trust intuition before we have proof?*

�֏   *How do we address the world community rather than limiting ourselves to any of our more circumscribed local audiences?*

✚   *How do we let life bring out the very best in us?*

✚   *How do we support our own and our colleagues' courage to speak out about the most important issues of our generation?*

Key Learning Points: Developing Self-Knowledge

Surpassing the limits that confine us entails taking risks, and sometimes it takes what others see in us to provide us with the confidence we need to take those risks. Has anyone ever told you that you were great at something you were insecure about? Their words probably gave you the confidence you needed to try a little harder, to become a little more than you otherwise would have. Because discovering our potential means exploring the unknown, it means taking chances, and sometimes it means making mistakes, but if we don't try, if we don't risk failure, we will not reach our potential.

After reading the preceding chapters, consider the following questions as you think about the risks you've taken:

✢   *When do you pause to reflect on your life and the factors that currently contribute to it? As you reflect, what do you find that is valuable? What can you do in the future that will be rewarding to you?*

✢   *Are you insecure or nervous about an aspect of your job? What would happen if you delved into this area?*

✢   *Think about the people around you. Is there something someone does that you think is valuable or unique? Have you told this person? Why or why not?*

✢   *Reflect on a risk that you've taken. What did you learn from it?*

✢   *Reflect on a mistake you've made. What did you learn from it? How does it help you in your life today?*

UNLEARNING
WHAT YOU THOUGHT
WAS SO

STRATFORD SHERMAN
What Strength Really Means

❧

JAY GALBRAITH
Learning to Live with Questions

❧

ROBERT W. EICHINGER
True Learning Is Often Slow

❧

R. ROOSEVELT THOMAS, JR.
The Impact of Paradigms on Change

21 STRATFORD SHERMAN

Stratford Sherman is a globally recognized authority on leadership, competitive response, and large-scale organizational change. After a two-decade career at Fortune *magazine, where he served on the board of editors, and many years as a sought-after speaker, he established an independent practice offering corporate advice and executive coaching. Sherman coauthored the bestselling study of Jack Welch's transformation of General Electric,* Control Your Destiny or Someone Else Will, *and contributed to the recent* Leading Beyond the Walls. *He is a member of the national advisory board of the Peter Drucker Foundation for Nonprofit Management, and chairman and cofounder of Lalibreria.com.*

What Strength Really Means

As I reflect on my life to date, it seems that the single greatest catalyst of personal growth was the process of making up my mind to propose to the woman who is now my wife. At the time of that decision, Meredith and I had been going out for three years. Three years of being in love and breaking up, loving and breaking up—on the whole it didn't seem to be going very well. At the time, I blamed the problem on what I perceived as Meredith's mood swings; I never considered the impact of my own dread of commitment. Eventually I decided we should separate for a while. My intention was to figure out whether to marry her or give her up for good. During those months, I entered a very intense process of introspection. Early on, the fundamental issue became clear: Meredith needed me to change, and change seemed impossible.

During this time of contemplation, I began to trace the origins of my way of life and, in particular, my resistance to change. My father had been a survivor of the Holocaust and a man who placed great emphasis on inner strength. He had raised me with the idea that to be a man, to be strong, was to be unchanging, like a great boulder in the middle of a raging river. The waters might rage, but the rock would never budge. Over time, I became rather accomplished in that method of living.

The benefits included firmness of character and an ability to withstand strength much greater than my own. As a reporter for a major business magazine, I often matched wits with chief executive officers of very large companies, people who ordinarily would intimidate a young person like me. Thanks to my father's gift of firmness, I felt at ease with them instead.

The idea of marital commitment, however, challenged this independent identity. It seemed to represent a tremendous, even intolerable, risk. After all, I knew who I was; if Meredith couldn't find a way to mesh with me, I figured, the result could only be disaster. My concern struck me as quite reasonable. After all, my parents had gotten divorced, and I had grown up amid ample evidence that marriages often fail, and painfully. I also hesitated to lose what had been a neatly compartmentalized relationship with Meredith, in which I was free to adore certain aspects of her nature, while refusing to deal with the aspects that made me uncomfortable.

As I came to recognize what a childish model of relationship this was, I also realized that the main obstacle we faced had nothing to do with Meredith: It was my own terror about what might lie beyond the chasm of change. I had entered the separation with a long, exquisitely detailed list of complaints about Meredith, precisely specifying every attribute that struck me as unbearable, every potential source of the conflict that, I imagined, might inevitably lead us to divorce. When at last I frankly considered the matter, though, I realized that my love for

Meredith was absolute. And in the context of that absolute, all the faults that I perceived in her added up to nothing.

The real issue began to emerge: I didn't want a nice person like Meredith to get stuck with a horrible guy like me. Once I finally stopped criticizing her, I had to acknowledge that she was right about my own need to evolve. Each of the issues that she had raised about my behavior began to seem worthy of consideration. Eventually the issue became clear: To marry Meredith, or indeed to be happy even without her, I would have to free myself of the long-festering feeling of being stuck, my stubborn insistence on preserving my every weakness and evasion. This was when, for the first time in my life, I recognized that I actually wanted to change. My love for this wonderful woman and the overwhelming strength of my desire to keep her in my life finally compelled me to launch a frontal assault on the idea that strength is about resisting change. I felt as if the very bedrock of my identity needed to be blown up. So . . . I blew it up.

The day finally came when I called up Meredith, took her out to dinner, and asked her—with what I thought was enormous charm—to marry me. Meredith didn't say yes. Yikes! I'd summoned the courage to go way out on a limb, and she left me there, trembling. After several weeks of testing my sincerity, trembling herself, she accepted my proposal. We have been married now for many years. We have two heavenly children. We have shared all the usual agonies and delights. And together we have experienced more happiness than either of us had ever expected of life.

In retrospect, my adulthood began with the decision to commit to change. The way I view the world shifted profoundly: Since then I have understood that strength of character is the ability to change when change is needed.

Not only my inner life but my professional life has blossomed as a result. From the time I was a boy, I had (like many members of the baby boom generation) been powerfully attracted to the idea of change—so long as it involved other people. Only after I began to experience change myself did my counsel begin to have value, and that value seems to have increased with time. Some years ago, I coauthored a book about the transformation of General Electric under Jack Welch. That work led to my active engagement in the dynamics of organizational transformation as a speaker, consultant, and executive coach. Over time, I have increasingly focused on the way large-scale organizational change interacts with, and depends upon, change at the very personal level of individual employees. Knowing something about change from within my own life has helped me deal with that issue, not as a theory, but as a living reality.

Today I try to help people in leadership positions understand and respect what people go through when they are asked to change. I am convinced that organizational transformation is not only a triumph of leadership but also the sum of individual acts of voluntary commitment. People need to understand their own need for change and decide independently that change is what they want. Without that commitment, shared by a great many individuals, organizational change can't reach beyond the narrow confines of reengineering. That's why I believe it is imperative that leaders understand what their employees want, what they believe, and how they feel. At work, as in marriage, voluntary commitment is the key to success.

QUESTIONS

⁜ *What is it that you're absolutely committed to?*

⁜ *How willing are you, in your own life, to change when change is needed?*

⁜ *Has your experience of change been reluctant and superficial, or has it been deep enough to strengthen your sense of ease and well-being?*

⁜ *In your relations with other people, are you honoring their need to make their own choices freely and without coercion?*

22 JAY GALBRAITH

Jay Galbraith is an internationally recognized expert on global organization design and founder of Galbraith Management Consultants. A former business school professor, he served on the faculty of the Sloan School of Management at MIT (Massachusetts Technical Institute) and the Wharton School at the University of Pennsylvania. He is an Affiliated Research Scientist at the Center for Effective Organizations at the University of Southern California and Professor Emeritus at the International Institute for Management Development (IMD) in Lausanne, Switzerland. The author of numerous books and articles, his most recent release is Designing Matrix Organizations that Actually Work *(Jossey-Bass, 2008).*

Learning to Live with Questions

I was not so much affected by any one incident or event as I was by a teacher who truly influenced how I think and question. I'd gone to engineering school, and I was a chemical engineer. Dissatisfied, I then went to graduate school, where I studied quantitative subjects such as economics, statistics, operations research, computers, and management. In graduate school I was also exposed to some nonquantitative disciplines. I took a course with James D. Thompson, who at the time was writing *Organizations in Action*, a landmark book for people involved in organization theory. In class each week, he would share a new chapter, and we would discuss the ideas it inspired in us.

Most of my professors were people who were selling their subject. I had a professor who was teaching Skinner's reinforcement theory, and according to him, this not only was the best way to understand reinforcement, but it was the only way. Thompson was different. The importance of a question to Professor Thompson lay not so much in delivering an answer but in the question itself. Unlike other teachers, Thompson would rarely answer the questions I came up with. Instead, he would clearly define what the question was and proceed to explore two or three positions that could be taken. The answer to my question was much less important to him than having me truly understand the question. This approach shaped my view on the world.

I was inspired to learn that the purely technical and quantitative answers weren't very satisfying. I understood that they are not what the world's problems are solely about; there is something more human. In my dealings now, I try to put several viewpoints together in an effective package that can help solve a problem. I don't produce a single answer on an issue.

These days I like to stay on the edge, questioning my own ideas and beliefs, whatever I hold as true. I like to look at complex issues and, as a result, often wind up arguing with my clients, who usually want to keep it simple. Sometimes the seduction of simplicity is just that—a seduction. Complexity can be intimidating, but by understanding what the questions are, a framework can be constructed to successfully deal with the issues at hand.

I have also learned to live with a question that has resulted from my research and consulting in organizations. During a consultation, I conduct interviews with the participants, and I have been struck by how partial their views are. They generally see only their part of the organization. After synthesizing a few interviews, I usually have a broad view of the company. This process has always reminded me of the story of the three blind men, each of whom was aware of only the part of the elephant he could touch. I used to think I could see the whole elephant.

But today I ask whether I can see the whole elephant or whether I am one more blind man.

QUESTIONS

✢ *Are there multiple viewpoints you can access in forming plans?*

✢ *Do you question your own perspective occasionally and try to see things from another perspective?*

23

ROBERT W. EICHINGER

*Robert Eichinger has more than forty-five years of experi-
ence teaching, consulting, and working in corporate positions. He now runs his own leadership development
product and publishing company, Lominger Limited, Inc.
Eichinger is a frequent speaker and workshop leader for
companies, associations, and professional groups. He has
coauthored a number of articles on executive development,
was on the adjunct staff of the Center for Creative Leadership, and codesigned the Leadership Architect® suite of
management and executive development tools, which is
being used at more than five hundred companies worldwide. Retired from active consulting, Eichinger is now
running and designing additional leadership development
products for Lominger Limited, Inc.*

True Learning Is Often Slow

For some reason, I grew up a professional critic. I was good at
finding fault with the projects and programs of others, at poking holes
in their balloons. As a matter of fact, I still am. I had some classic de-
bates with some of my instructors in college. I guess I thought I could
get my head higher if I could make other people's lower. I was bright
and brash, and it wasn't that my criticisms were necessarily wrong; they
were just constant and overwhelming.

Moving straight out of graduate school and into a consulting firm in Houston, I found myself in my first real job. Full of vigor and book learning, I was ready to change the world. About six months into this new job, my boss, who would be an important mentor to me later, called me in for a six-month review. "Bob," he said, "you are obviously bright and talented. Someday you might make a good consultant. But for now, we would appreciate it if you would keep your criticisms of what other consultants are doing inside the firm to yourself. Frankly, you have no credibility with us yet. You have no right to criticize anyone because you haven't done anything yet. You have come up with about ten good ideas since you have been here. Pick one. Do it. Make it a success. Then we might be interested in what you have to say about the ideas of others. In the meantime, shut up and do something. And by the way, if you can't take something and make it work, your time here will be short."

The principle I needed to learn? He who criticizes must be willing to put himself on the line first to gain the right to criticize others. I did pick something. I made it a success. I curtailed my criticisms and stayed with this consulting firm for eight years. Interestingly, my need to criticize others diminished.

Nine years later, I was corporate head of management development in a Fortune 500 company. My boss called me in one day and said, "The chairman wants to have a leadership model for the company. Go find one." I was excited! This would be my first real exposure to the chairman. I did my homework: I read all the relevant literature, established benchmarks, and went to a leadership conference. I chose the top ten leadership models available at the time and created a great presentation. I had slides (forty-five altogether!) for each model. Method? Author(s)? Findings? I knew them. I had a group of summary slides on the common elements of the ten models and how they differed. I was versed in the pros and cons of each. Rehearsing, I thought, "This is a good piece of work." My professors would be proud. I was ready to go.

My boss was a hands-off type. He didn't want to look at what I had put together before we presented it to the chairman. I didn't sleep the night before. On the day of my presentation, in the boardroom no less, I began with a brief introduction. I described Kotter's model, then went on to Bennis. I was about to go on to Bass when the chairman said, "Bob, is the rest of your presentation like this? Are you going to tell me your opinion of what the leadership model should be for this organization?"

I froze. I looked desperately toward my boss for support. Nothing. I replied that I had read all the literature and was presenting what I had found so that he (the chairman) could decide what he wanted for the company. He said, "I could get a review of the literature for a lot less money than I'm paying you. I want to know what you recommend. I'm not interested in how you got there. If you want to continue working here, have that ready next Wednesday at 3 p.m." He got up and walked out of the boardroom nine minutes into our scheduled hour. "That wasn't a very good start with the chairman," my boss said flatly. Quite an understatement, I thought. He then added, "It's time to put up or shut up. See you next Wednesday."

I went back to work. This time I talked to a number of leaders in the organization about what they thought they needed to be successful. I met with the head of strategic planning to see what she thought the organization was facing in going forward. I talked to my boss about what he thought. Then I went back to my research to find the model.

Synthesizing all of the new information, I came up with eleven factors or "competencies." I defined each of them, performed a "Why might this factor be important around here?" analysis, and again was ready to go. Wednesday came. This time I had fifteen slides: two introductory slides, eleven for the eleven factors, one on why the plan I was proposing would work, and one conclusion. I gave my presentation. The chairman made one change in one of the factors, then said, "Good work. Implement the model." And we did. It was used in that organization for the next eleven years. I stayed for seven more years. The principle I learned? Be a person who adds value. Parroting, no matter how academically sound, isn't of value in the real world.

Eight more years passed, and I had a very hands-on boss. He wanted to see all my work. He was a very good organizational politician, which meant that I and others on his staff seldom got into trouble because he always had useful input; he would edit and rehearse and add value to our work. He and I developed the first enterprise-wide employee survey. My task was to put together the questionnaire. I read the literature, set benchmarks, talked to some questionnaire vendors, interviewed the eight general managers to see what information they needed, and created a questionnaire.

Then a crisis emerged—my boss announced he was leaving. We had the party and said our good-byes. The survey was scheduled to start in two weeks, and the new boss had just come in. I scheduled some time with her. I told her I needed her to review and approve the questions so we could go to print. She said, "If I need to review the questions, I don't need you. If you can't design a survey that adds value and works, I'll get someone else who can." This was becoming a very clear message.

I went back to look at the questions myself. There's no doubt I had become lazy with my previous boss because I knew he would catch any gross political errors. I had put in some questionable items that were of interest to me but that I was sure he would challenge and probably take out. I took most of those out myself. I had two colleagues look at the items, made a couple of changes, and implemented the questionnaire. It was successful and is still being used today, with some new items added each year. The principle I learned this time? Stand up and be counted; be as self-sufficient as possible; do complete work the first time.

These lessons span eighteen years—too long, I suppose, but I am a slow learner. It took three shocks to my system, but these lessons are now firmly embedded in my mind:

1.   Add value to everything you do.
2.   Be as self-sufficient as possible in what you do.
3.   Form a viewpoint on key issues. Stand up and be counted!
4.   Criticize sparingly.

QUESTIONS

‡   *What does it mean to add value?*

‡   *What does it take to form a viewpoint on an issue?*

‡   *Why is it important to criticize sparingly?*

24 R. ROOSEVELT THOMAS, JR.

Over the past twenty-five years, Dr. R. Roosevelt Thomas, Jr., has been at the forefront of developing and implementing innovative concepts and strategies for maximizing organizational and individual potential through Diversity Management. Founder of the American Institute for Managing Diversity (AIMD), a nonprofit research and education enterprise, and Roosevelt Thomas Consulting & Training, Dr. Thomas is the author of six published books and numerous articles. In 1998, the National Academy of Human Resources elected Dr. Thomas as a Fellow. He has also been recognized in The Wall Street Journal *as a top business consultant, cited by* Human Resource Executive *as one of HR's Most Influential People, and awarded the "Distinguished Contribution to Human Resource Development" Award by the American Society for Training and Development. Dr. Thomas has served as a consultant to numerous Fortune 500 companies, corporations, professional firms, government entities, nonprofit organizations, and academic institutions. Contact Roosevelt at* RThomas@rthomasconsulting.com *and* www.rthomasconsulting.com.

The Impact of Paradigms on Change

Over the years, I have been fortunate to present to audiences of senior executives, managers, and individual contributors, and to have received favorable responses to my ideas on diversity management. These warm receptions, however, have not generated corresponding adoptions of my prescriptions.

A panel experience some years back reflected this phenomenon. Following my comments as moderator, each panelist began his or her presentation with complimentary remarks about my work. Yet, descriptions of their activities revealed little—if any—connection to my thoughts about diversity management.

As the panelists greeted members of the audience individually after the general discussion, I saw a woman lingering in the back of the crowd and smiling at me. Her smile suggested that we knew each other, but I could not remember her face or name. When she finally inched her way to the stage, she said: "Hello, Roosevelt. You keep saying the same thing over and over and over. It really must be frustrating to hear people declare themselves as followers of your work, and then describe initiatives that bear no relation to your thinking."

I responded by laughing for several seconds as I thought about the truth of her comment. She continued, "But don't stop; we'll hear you eventually."

I have thought about this woman's encouragement from time to time, and pondered possible reasons for the disconnect she cited. The answers eluded me for quite a while. Recently, however, I have concluded that one explanation might be that my dominant diversity paradigm is different from those of many to whom I typically present, and that their paradigms might predispose them to distance themselves from my thinking—even as they find it provocative, interesting, and sound. Implementing my ideas would require shifting long-held paradigms or—at a minimum—going against the grain of their mind-sets and predispositions. This may explain why they applaud my work and then fail to move forward with change and implementation.

This insight has come not as a result of a cognitive epiphany but rather as a result of observing my personal responses as I bump against my own paradigms, both current and remembered. I believe that this insight can be helpful to anyone with the responsibility of influencing another's behavior, whether as a leader, manager, coach, or mentor.

THE AIRPORT BATHROOM PARADIGM

Not long ago, I passed through the new airport in Jacksonville, Florida, and used one of the men's rooms. As I prepared to wash my hands, I could not locate the wash basins. Looking around more intently and beginning to feel inept, I still saw no basins. I retraced my steps, thinking I had inadvertently missed them. Still, no basins in sight.

Finally, I noticed a gray marble slab, but still no basins. I then sighted the water faucets over the slab, and deduced that individuals were to wash their hands and then allow the water to drain into a trench behind the slab.

Once I realized all of this, my head was spinning. Questions abounded. "Why?!" Is this less expensive?" "Is this more sanitary?" "Is this more aesthetic?" "Why?!!"

At one point, I literally became angry and almost went looking for the airport manager. I wanted to give him a piece of my mind and to register a complaint, and ask why he had abandoned wash basins. They had worked fine for years. Why the change?!

Realizing that my Jacksonville experience stemmed from the reality that the new airport clashed with my paradigm about airport bathrooms and wash basins, I then wondered what other paradigms have predisposed me to certain expectations and behaviors. Two came readily to mind: The Spaghetti Paradigm and the Pencil Grip Paradigm.

THE SPAGHETTI PARADIGM

I grew up with my mother and grandmother, who regularly cooked spaghetti. They did so in a way not often seen today. I think they fried it with onions, peppers, and tomato sauce. I loved the spaghetti of my mother and grandmother.

My wife also cooks spaghetti, and I enjoy the way she prepares it, although it differs from my growing-up experience. Not long after we married, she cooked some pasta dishes. I immediately informed her that I did not like these preparations. She asked how I could eat spaghetti and yet not like pasta. I told her it was simple: "I eat spaghetti, not pasta." She declared in bewilderment, "Spaghetti is pasta!"

For me, this was not true. Growing up, spaghetti was spaghetti, not pasta. Not one time had I ever heard anything about pasta. My spaghetti paradigm in no way predisposed me to eat pasta.

THE PENCIL GRIP PARADIGM

My mother taught me to write at a pre-school age. I learned well and received accolades from my kindergarten and early elementary school teachers. Everything was fine until one of my peers derided me for holding my pencil "funny."

When I told my mother, she replied that she had been so pleased and excited that I was writing that she forgot to notice my grip. Stated differently, my grip paradigm differed from that formally prescribed for young students. She laughed about it.

To this day, I do not hold writing instruments correctly. I have come to think of it as a "special" manifestation of the fact that my mother taught me to write, and also of our relationship. She was proud she had taught me to write, albeit with an improper grip.

And I remain proud to have been taught by my mother. I am grateful to her for sending me off to a good start, although I am not certain that I ever told her.

LESSONS GLEANED FROM MY PERSONAL PARADIGMS

As I have reflected on these paradigm clashes and my reaction to them, I have identified lessons that make it easier for me to feel empathy for, not impatience with, those who resist implementing my ideas. The lessons also reinforce my commitment to identifying ways to help others make the transition from familiar but dated diversity management paradigms to those more likely to succeed. I share these lessons below.

One, modifying a comfortable paradigm can be difficult. In each of the paradigm clashes noted here, I consistently have resisted change. I still refuse to eat "pasta" despite the fact that I eat spaghetti. And I still hold my pencils "incorrectly."

Two, clashes between one person's paradigm and that of another can be deeply disturbing and even threatening. As I searched for the wash basins, I started to question myself and to wonder whether I was inept in some way.

My reactions were similar to that of a chief diversity officer encountering for the first time my definition of diversity as differences and similarities that can characterize a mixture of *any* kind. My more expansive undergirding paradigm clashed with her paradigm that defined diversity as being primarily about race and gender. She responded by stating her beliefs about diversity and asking, "Am I right or is Roosevelt wrong?" The differences in our explicit statements and their implicit underlying paradigms threatened her and caused her to fear she might be wrong. She subsequently became defensive and missed an opportunity to explore the compatibility and utility of each definition.

Three, paradigm clashes can lead to paradigm shock characterized by emotional and physical stress. My reaction to the lack of wash basins provides an example. For a few minutes, I experienced frustration, self-doubt, and anger to a degree that I find surprising in retrospect. I suffered from shock that my basic paradigm around airport bathrooms and wash basins had been violated.

The notion of paradigm shock explains the reaction of an African American to my claims that race and gender were not the only types of workforce diversity. He asked in disbelief, "Are you saying that the discomfort experienced by white males as a result of being in a non-preferred function is comparable to the stress and pain I suffer from racial discrimination?" When I responded that it could be, he stated loudly, "I don't think so!"

Four, paradigms can cause one to deny reality. Without a doubt, spaghetti is a form of pasta. Yet, because of my paradigm regarding spaghetti, I am extremely reluctant to admit this reality and to deal with its implications—especially the one that suggests my reasoning for not eating pasta is absurd.

This propensity to deny reality also is seen in organizational leaders who have difficulty accepting that diversity encompasses more than workforce diversity. They ignore the Complex Organizations literature addressing the "diversity" of functions and lines of business in an organization, clinging instead to a "diversity as race and gender" paradigm that will not allow them to deal with evidence to the contrary.

Five, paradigms linger. Long after they have been modified or dismantled, their influence persists. Consider the following case of a senior white male who approached me from the perspective of a dated paradigm.

Years ago, I suggested to a group of senior managers that, in anticipation of projected demographic shifts, they should develop a diversity management capability before they had to do so. Following my presentation, a white male cautioned me about the "have to do so" language. He counseled that white males did not "have to do anything" and might be offended by my language.

In paradigm-speak, he was saying, "As I listened to you, I felt a tug from the 'white man is superior and in control paradigm' that prescribes that 'black males' must show respect to white males. Your 'have to do so' comment violates this paradigm and will undercut your potential for fostering change. Now, I know that this paradigm no longer prevails, but I am sharing with you what I honestly am feeling."

I perceived this man to be a person of good intent. He simply got caught up in the lingering tendencies of a dying paradigm. If asked about this paradigm, he would have disowned it and expressed delight that it was dying—even as he swayed to its lingering traces.

Six. Given the power of our paradigms and the disorientation and discomfort that accompany changing them, change leaders must proceed with empathy and persistence, rejecting any inclination toward annoyance or impatience. Paradigm change is neither an easy nor a short-term project.

IMPLICATIONS FOR LEADING CHANGE

These six lessons hold significant—indeed critical—implications for myself and other change agents—mentors, leaders, managers, coaches—anyone attempting to influence the behavior of another.

First, change agents must explicitly work the paradigm arena. If as a change agent, you want to go from point A to point B, you must identify the paradigms undergirding each. Then, you must determine the gap between the undergirding paradigms and work to minimize A's, while fostering B's. If the gap between the two undergirding paradigms is significant, any movement toward status B will be difficult and challenging to sustain. By undergirding paradigm, I mean those that cause each position to be viewed as desirable.

Yet, change agents typically do not address paradigms. The diversity field is a good example. Diversity practitioners typically detail plans along with supporting rationales and then advocate vigorously for their recommendations, but do generally not dwell on whether the related undergirding paradigms are facilitators or hindrances. Only recently have we started to give prominence to the importance of paradigms in the diversity arena.

The *second* implication is that change agents must help individuals and organizations through paradigm shifts and related clashes and shocks. This clearly was needed for me in the Jacksonville airport.

I would have appreciated some education or warning before entering the men's room. In paradigm-speak, the message could have been as follows: "Mr. Thomas, we know you have an entrenched paradigm around wash basins in bathrooms; however, when you enter our washroom, you will see a configuration that clashes with your existing mind-set. Be assured, with respect to basic functionality, you will be satisfied—albeit in unfamiliar surroundings. For your information the paradigm shift has been to one emphasizing conservation—a major theme of our new airport." (Conservation is noted here for illustrative purposes. In reality, I don't know what the new airport's paradigm is.) Such help would have diminished my anger and frustration.

A *third* implication is that we need to assist beyond the apparent success of the paradigm shift. Since traces of old paradigms can linger, change agents must be prepared to deal with lingering influences from displaced paradigms.

In the airport example, this would mean reminders as I returned to the site on subsequent trips. The reminders might be, "Welcome back, Mr. Thomas. We just want to remind you of our new bathroom arrangements . . . " This would help reorient me to the new configuration after intermediary experiences with traditional airports. Without this follow-up assistance, I would run once again significant risk of paradigm shock.

Finally, if the paradigm shift is right *and* important, the change agent should be prepared to persevere. This was the message the woman lingering in the back of the crowd wanted to deliver to me. In paradigm-speak she stated, "Roosevelt, I know you must grow weary from saying the same thing over and over with less than proportionate success. You must understand that you are advocating the changing of some deeply entrenched paradigms, and that significant effort and time will be required. Persevere!"

In essence, she stopped by to remind me that I was dealing not just with change, but with paradigms as well.

The notion of "importance" is critical. With respect to pasta, for health reasons I will not be consuming much. So, it becomes relatively unimportant for me to abandon my "Spaghetti is spaghetti" mind-set. Similarly, the proper way to grip a pencil has become a moot issue for me. I literally have written entire books manually with an improper grip.

On the other hand, in an increasingly global and complex world, moving people from seeing diversity as race and gender in the workforce to seeing it as differences and similarities that can characterize *any* mixture in *any* setting and in *any* geographical location is becoming increasingly important. This type of paradigm shift merits attention and perseverance.

My experience with discomfort in dealing with personal paradigm "disconnects" has led me to pause and ask several questions when facing decisions about new or different realities. Answering these questions can be time-consuming and disconcerting. Yet I believe that all who seek to change behaviors, or respond to expectations to change their own, will find that the time invested in posing and answering these questions will help the necessary paradigm change process to go more smoothly.

QUESTIONS

✷ *Can I identify two or three of the key paradigms determining my life?*

✷ *If I cannot identify significant paradigms, how can I become aware of them? Is the issue significant enough that I am willing to make the effort?*

✷ *How can I make certain that the influences of my key paradigms remain current and appropriate, and do not disconnect me from reality?*

✷ *Once I have identified and examined my key paradigms, how can I use this knowledge to enhance my personal and professional life?*

Key Learning Points:
Unlearning What You Thought Was So

Now this is a hard one! Why, if learning takes such energy, commitment, and resources, would anyone want to spend more time and energy in the "unlearning" process? The answer, of course, is to grow. This kind of "unlearning" growth is particularly difficult because it demands that the individual let go. As Peter Vaill said in *Learning as a Way of Being*, "We do not need competency skills for this life. We need incompetency skills, the skills of being effective beginners."

After reading the preceding chapters, consider your experience with "unlearning" and reflect on the following questions:

‡ *When have you had to back up and relearn something you believed as true? How did this happen?*

‡ *What are some coping mechanisms you used or can use to overcome the feelings of inadequacy that come with unlearning?*

‡ *What are some behaviors individuals can develop to ensure that they are learning all they can, even in familiar environments?*

‡ *How can being open to new learnings help in situations where diversity presents itself?*

PAIN IS A
GREAT TEACHER

MARSHALL GOLDSMITH
The Person in the Mirror

❦

FREDERIC M. HUDSON
My Wake-up Call

❦

BEVERLY KAYE
Making the Flat Side Round

❦

DAVID M. NOER
The Gain Is Worth the Pain

❦

CHARLES E. DWYER
What Do You Do When Things Go Wrong?

25 MARSHALL GOLDSMITH

Marshall Goldsmith is a world authority in helping success-ful leaders get even better by achieving positive, lasting change in behavior: for themselves, their people, and their teams. In November 2009, he was ranked as one of the fifteen most influential business thinkers in the world in a study (involving 35,000 respondents) published by The (London) Times *and* Forbes. *Dr. Goldsmith's books have sold more than one million copies and have been translated into more than twenty-five languages. His* New York Times *bestseller,* What Got You Here Won't Get You There, *is a* Wall Street Journal #1 *bestseller and Harold Longman Award Winner for Business Book of the Year. Marshall is one of a select few advisors who have been asked to work with more than 120 CEOs and their management teams. His newest book is* MOJO: How to Get It, How to Keep It, and How to Get It Back When You Lose It. *Contact Marshall at* marshall@marshallgoldsmith.com *and* www.marshallgoldsmithlibrary.com.

The Person in the Mirror

As a Ph.D. student at UCLA in the early 1970s, I had a self-image of being "hip" and "cool." I believed I was intensely involved in deep human understanding, self-actualization, and the uncovering of profound wisdom. Early in my Ph.D. program, I was one of thirteen students in a class led by a wise teacher, Bob Tannenbaum. Bob had come up with the term *sensitivity training*, had published the most widely distributed article to appear in the *Harvard Business Review*, and was a full professor. He was a very important person in our department at UCLA. He was also a great guy.

In Bob's class, we were encouraged to discuss anything we wanted to discuss. I began by talking about people in Los Angeles. For three full weeks I gave monologues about how "screwed up" people in Los Angeles were. "They wear these $78 sequined blue jeans and drive gold Rolls-Royces; they are plastic and materialistic; all they care about is impressing others; and they really do not understand what is deep and important in life." (It was easy for me to be an expert on the people of Los Angeles. I had, after all, grown up in a small town in Kentucky.)

One day, after listening to me babble for three weeks, Bob looked at me quizzically and asked, "Marshall, who are you talking to?"

"I am speaking to the group," I answered.

"Who in the group are you talking to?"

"Well, I am talking to everybody," I replied, not quite knowing where he was headed with this line of questioning.

"I don't know if you realize this," Bob said, "but each time you have spoken, you have looked at only one person. You have addressed your comments toward only one person. And you seem interested in the opinion of only one person. Who is that person?"

"That is interesting. Let me think about it," I replied. Then (after careful consideration) I said, "You?"

He said, "That's right, me. There are twelve other people in this room. Why don't you seem interested in any of them?"

Now that I had dug myself into a hole, I decided to dig even deeper. I said, "You know, Dr. Tannenbaum, I think you can understand the true significance of what I am saying. I think you can truly understand how 'screwed up' it is to try to run around and impress people all the time. I believe you have a deep understanding of what is really important in life."

Bob looked at me and said, "Marshall, is there any chance that for the last three weeks all you have been trying to do is impress me?"

I was amazed at Bob's obvious lack of insight! "Not at all!" I declared. "I don't think you have understood one thing I have said! I have been explaining to you how screwed up it is to try to impress other people. I think you have totally missed my point, and frankly, I am a little disappointed in your lack of understanding!"

He looked at me, scratched his beard, and concluded, "No. I think I understand."

I looked around and saw twelve people scratching their faces and thinking, "Yes. We understand."

Suddenly, I had a deep dislike for Dr. Tannenbaum. I devoted a lot of energy to figuring out his psychological problems and understanding why he was confused. But after six months, it finally dawned on me that the person with the issue wasn't him. It wasn't even the people in Los Angeles. The person with the real issue was me. I finally looked in the mirror and said, "You know, old Dr. Tannenbaum was exactly right."

Two of the great lessons I began to understand from this experience were (1) that it is much easier to see our problems in others than it is to see them in ourselves, and (2) even though we may be able to deny our problems to ourselves, they may be very obvious to the people who are observing us.

There is almost always a discrepancy between the self we think we are and the self the rest of the world sees in us. The lesson I learned (and strive in my professional work to help others understand) is that often the rest of the world has a more accurate perspective than we do. If we can stop, listen, and think about what others see in us, we have a great opportunity. We can compare the self that we want to be with the self we are presenting to the rest of the world. We can then begin to make the real changes needed to align our stated values with our actual behavior.

I have told this story at least three hundred times, and I have thought about it more frequently than I have told it. Often when I become self-righteous, preachy, holier than thou, or angry about some perceived injustice, I eventually realize that the issue is not with the other person or people. The issue is usually in me.

Today I work mostly with executives in large organizations. I help them develop a profile of desired leadership behavior. Then I provide them with confidential feedback, which allows them to compare their behavior (as perceived by others) with their profile of desired behavior. I try to help them deal with this feedback in a positive way, to learn from it, and (eventually) to become a good role model for the desired leadership behavior in their organization. Although I am supposed to be a "coach," very little of my coaching involves "sharing my wisdom." Most of it involves helping my clients learn from the people around them. In this way, the lesson I learned from Bob Tannenbaum has not only helped me in my personal life; it has helped shape the course of my professional life.

QUESTIONS

✢ *Can you see in yourself what others see in you, or do you see in others what you don't want to see in yourself?*

✢ *What really bothers you about the "rest of the world"?*

✢ *Is there a chance that some of your concerns may be a reflection of your problems, not theirs?*

✢ *How can honest feedback from others help you in aligning your values with your behavior?*

26 FREDERIC M. HUDSON

Frederic Hudson is an educator, writer, trainer, and recognized adult change expert. He is widely respected for his contributions to the fields of adult development, career transition planning, and human and organization development. As a Rockefeller and Danforth Fellow, Hudson earned his doctorate at Columbia University and taught at Colby College and the University of San Francisco. From 1974 through 1986, he was the founding president of the Fielding Institute. In 1987 he founded The Hudson Institute of Santa Barbara, a training center focused on coaching and renewal in the workplace and for the individual. Hudson was named "Executive Coach of the Year" by AT&T, "The Best Seminar Leader We've Ever Had" by 3M, and "Life/Work Balance Coach" by Harley-Davidson. He is author of The Adult Years: Mastering the Art of Self-Renewal.

My Wake-up Call

My life course was shaped indelibly by a traumatic event in my childhood. I share this story here because it vividly represents the message of my life: always have a vision, formulate a plan, and lean into the wind.

On August 23, 1943, when I was nine years old, I awakened in silent terror. I was unable to move any part of my body except my eyes. My muscles seemed frozen, and my voice was silenced. Although I had gone to bed as a walking, talking, wiggling boy, I woke up the next day paralyzed with polio. Neither my legs nor my arms would respond to my desperate efforts to move, and my neck and jaw were as rigid as rocks. My breathing was panicked, and I felt pain everywhere. In the 1940s, polio was a dreaded epidemic of unidentified origin for which there was no means of prevention and no real medical treatment. Many who contracted it died; others went through life in braces and wheelchairs.

The next thing I remember was lying on the backseat of my parents' car as they drove me thirty miles to a hospital in Syracuse, New York. That journey was unbelievably painful. I was sicker than I had ever felt in my life, and I felt a helplessness and fear I had never experienced before. "What will happen to me?" I pondered. "Am I going to die? Will I ever see my family again? It isn't fair!" That day remains vivid in my mind, like a screeching siren I can't turn off.

At the hospital, I was placed on a very hard bed with no pillow, in a quarantined ward. I spent my waking moments staring upward at the ceiling—my only option—feeling totally helpless.

A wise nurse named Susan spent lots of time with me. Quiet and caring, she visited me frequently and told me many things. Her main message was something like this: "Your future, Frederic, is hidden on the ceiling, and you are the only one who can find it. Look for what you will be doing as you grow up. It's all up there. Will you be a track star, a tennis player, a scientist? Will you be going on trips to faraway places? Will you be going to summer camps and swimming? Will you go to college and become someone special? Will you marry and have a family? Frederic, all you have to do is study the ceiling. When you see your future, it will start to happen!"

That's all she ever talked about—my future. I spent hours and then days and months searching for snapshots of my future in the maze on that dirty ceiling above my immobile body. The first vision I saw had me running and playing and active again. I saw myself as a young deer leaping effortlessly through a forest. After a while, I had only to lift up my eyes and I would see myself bouncing along, alive with graceful movements and amazing speed. Then I saw myself having friends, laughing again, and climbing trees. After a few months of ceiling gazing, I pictured myself going to college and becoming a husband and father someday. I even envisioned myself as a doctor.

Susan convinced me that if I would keep rehearsing my vision on the ceiling, sooner or later my body would begin to move again and make it all happen. I never doubted her. At the very time when my body was at its all-time low, I trusted her to coach me toward my highest self. Knowing my eyeballs were my only moving part, she brought a projector into my room and flashed stories and pictures on the ceiling for me to consider as I pondered my future. She projected a checkerboard and taught me how to play checkers and chess as she facilitated a learning environment for my future. She would read me books while instructing me to find my life in the patterns overhead. She brought me music to listen to, as well as recordings of famous books. Slowly but surely I began to feel the world of sound and sight open up before me.

She obtained my school assignments for the fourth and fifth grades and tutored me without my even knowing I was doing schoolwork. Honoring my wish to become a medical doctor, Susan procured the graduate bulletins of Yale, Harvard, and Columbia medical schools. She deciphered the undergraduate prerequisites and modified the learning process to suit someone my age. Before I left the hospital, she had engaged me with advanced mathematics, French, philosophy, and English literature. I felt so privileged to be learning so much that I imagined that everyone in my class was in a hospital somewhere—with polio—learning from nurses like Susan!

Before contracting polio, I had not been much of a student. My family was struggling to survive the Depression and World War II, and I was squeezed in between a brother a year older and a sister a year younger. Life was a day-by-day scramble. My father worked in a pharmaceutical manufacturing plant, and my mother worked part-time as a clerk in a drugstore.

But during my months in the hospital, in my desperate physical condition, time was all I had, and I wanted to learn everything I could. I wanted to become everything I could become. And I believed that what I envisioned on the ceiling would come to pass. Everything I imagined seemed possible, and what did I have to lose? Except for me, the room was silent and empty. I had no radio, and TV had not yet been invented. Thank God! It took a lot of silence for me to find my soul and invent my future.

One day, as I was entranced in a forest walk along the cracks in the ceiling, I felt a wiggle in the toes of my left foot. It was not much, but it was everything. I could move my toes, a little. When Susan made her rounds, she assured me that this was the beginning of my future unfolding, not merely my getting well, but my visions being realized. She said my strength would slowly return up my legs, my backbone and arms, and finally my upper neck and chin. "You are now in training," she would say, "so practice moving your foot for the rest of the month." She tied a string to my toes up through an eyelet she screwed into the ceiling (I winced when she made a hole in the secret garden of my mind's eye), and secured a small bell to it. "Ring the bell," she insisted, and I did, having no knowledge of Pavlov and his dog.

I was astounded that Susan knew the path to my recovery and transformation. She placed twine around my foot, up through a pulley (screwed into the ceiling!), and down to a handle on a casement window to my right. "Frederic," she whispered, "make the window go open and closed until it makes so much noise that every nurse on the floor scolds you." This was high motivation for a nine-year-old, and although I was unable to move my foot for weeks or months, my attention was completely riveted to doing so. In time, it happened, and only years later did I learn that all the nurses were instructed by Susan to rush into my room to complain royally.

In time, my room looked like a gymnasium, with ropes going in various directions to engage my awakening limbs with necessary exercise. I loved my room, and I had no intention of ever leaving. As ugly and bereft as it was, it was my secret garden. Never before had I been so awake, alive, and ready to soar. The last parts to cooperate were my neck and upper chest, and although I still can't touch my chin to my chest, I have been eternally grateful for everything I learned and became in my recovery. I now walk, run, play tennis, and live without any noticeable deficit.

The hardest thing I ever did was leave that room. I cried in anguish as my wheelchair left the hospital for my uncle's farm, where I was quarantined to learn to walk again. My loneliness there was punctuated by the deadly, daily visits of an orthopedic nurse who made me exercise, without any of the mentoring Susan had provided. It was months before I could walk, but when I did, I had a vision of where I was going and how I would get there. I had a purpose, and I planned my life around it.

I did not fully grasp what Susan had taught me until mid-life, when I was struggling mightily with my path and my life course. By then I had shifted from becoming a doctor of medicine to becoming a doctor of philosophy. After earning a Ph.D. at Columbia University, one of the schools Susan had recommended, I became a professor of philosophy at Colby College in Maine and then at the University of San Francisco. I also became a husband and a father. I wrote some books, became a good public speaker, and arrived at the goals I had envisioned with Susan.

In my late thirties, when my youth felt spent, I thought my life was over. I was out of vision. After much soul searching, I returned to what I had learned from Susan—to be visionary and responsible for my own future. Since I remained Susan's close friend until her death in 1989, I phoned to get her advice. This is what she said: "Yesterday's dreams are not always tomorrow's promises, Frederic. Gaze at the sky above you as if you were in the hospital again, and get a new fix on where you are going, and why. What we need at midlife is not always what we wanted when we were young. Find the fire, the passion, the hope that belongs to you. It's always up there, ready to be loaned to the right person at the right time." I cried with joy.

So again I learned, painfully, to gaze at the ceiling of my life to find new paths into my future. I tell my story so every reader can benefit from Susan's simple wisdom:

Envision how you want your life to unfold.

- Look for your best choices.

- Trust your vision. All anyone has is time. Make the most of it.

- Create a detailed plan to get you from here to there.

- Take responsibility for your life course: Time manage every detail.

- Find the best resources available for empowering your future. Network, train, travel, seek, adventure.

- Learn how to learn, unlearn, and relearn. Make learning your central business.

- Live on the outer edge of your reach, not on the inner edge of your security.

QUESTIONS

✤ *Gaze at your ceiling. What do you see for yourself?*

✤ *What actions can you take to get there?*

✤ *How can you play the role of Susan and help others gain a vision?*

27 BEVERLY KAYE

Beverly Kaye is an internationally recognized authority on career issues, and on retention and engagement in the workplace. As founder and CEO of Career Systems International, and a bestselling author on workplace performance, Dr. Kaye has worked with a host of organizations to establish cutting-edge, award-winning talent development solutions. Her first book, Up Is Not The Only Way, *became a classic. In it she foresaw the effects that leaner, flatter organizations would have on individual careers and the subsequent need for workers to take charge of their own careers. With the fourth edition of* Love 'Em or Lose 'Em: Getting Good People to Stay *(Berrett-Koehler, 2008), a bestseller she coauthored, Bev once again proved to be a pioneer in addressing one of the most pressing workplace problems of the twenty-first century: retaining and engaging employees. In her follow-up companion bestseller,* Love It, Don't Leave It: 26 Ways to Get What You Want at Work *(Berrett-Koehler, 2003), she shows employees how they can find greater satisfaction in their current work lives.*

Making the Flat Side Round

Kirkegaard had it right when he said that life must be lived forward but can only be understood backward. I translate this: If only I had known then what I know now! One incident that changed my view of myself and gave me the platform I still stand on today almost proved to be my own undoing.

It happened at UCLA. I had completed my coursework and had to defend my dissertation. My subject was organizational career development. I had selected a committee I thought knew me, liked me, and would be gentle. I had also selected, as was my style, a dissertation approach I could get my arms around. It would be relatively clean, clear, quick (I hoped), and something that would fit my style, which was "take action," "move quickly," "work hard," and "check it off the list"—a Jersey girl approach.

As I now understand backward, my learning style was limited. I memorized thoroughly, studied long and hard, and did everything I could to get extra credit. I didn't see myself as naturally smart, and therefore everything took more time, more pain. But I was a diligent student and knew what to do to get through. I knew my learning comfort areas and boundaries.

And unfortunately, my committee knew them too.

My dissertation approach was rejected. I had been so sure of myself that I had been taping it for my folks. The committee told me to start again and described the approach I should take. I now had a cassette filled with my begging them to reconsider and not "do this to me at the END of my education."

That, of course, clinched it for them. And for me.

They asked me to do phenomenological research: grounded theory. They said they saw my flat side; I operated from my intuition and not from a theory base. I didn't know what they were asking me to do, but I was sure I would not like it. And I didn't, not one bit. Nor did I have any idea how to do it, even though I read Glaser and Strauss's *Grounded Theory* several times.

Phenomenological research requires that you develop your own theory. You investigate a phenomenon and collect data. When your theory holds all your data, you've got it. Three times I tried. Three times I struck out. Sitting with data was just not me. Sitting and thinking was just not me. *Sitting* was definitely not me!

Two things kept me going: My mom (when she saw how upset I was) said, "Why not quit?" (and then I knew I couldn't), and one of the professors on my committee said, "Bev, if you hang in there, this will be your career development." I didn't know what that meant, but I knew it was an important message.

I finally got smart. Out of desperation (and loneliness), I hired a friend to sit and listen to me talk about the data I had collected. As I talked and as she listened, the theory began to bubble up. And when I presented my findings, the committee finally said, "By George, she's got it!"

That theory became my first book; that book led to my consulting practice and to the tools and materials I have since developed both on my own and with colleagues. That theory, now updated, is with me today in all I teach, and in all I teach others to teach. It still guides my thinking; it grounds me and directs me.

So what did I learn? I learned that I needed to be pushed out of my comfort zone to really learn what I could do. I recognized that I was caught in what David Kolb would term two and only two learning styles: "active experimentation" and "concrete experience." If I were ever to truly develop, I had to add "reflective observation" and "abstract conceptualization" to my bag.

I've often thought that if the committee had described it to me that way, I might not have fought it as I did. If they had drawn that learning cycle and explained how this was going to "round me out," I would not have suffered so much. I would have known where they were trying to help me go. Maybe.

I learned that if one is to have a platform, one has to come to that platform in one's own time and in one's one way. And when it is truly yours, you stand on firm ground. From that firm ground, you can do almost anything.

I learned that collaboration (for me) is sweet, that my best thinking is done in concert with others, and that there is nothing wrong with asking for help. I've used that lesson to grow my business, my practice, and my approach to living.

I learned (and have had to relearn more than once) that it is when the ground turns to quicksand that the most valuable learning and most valuable and enduring growth is about to happen. Oh, that there were an easier way!

QUESTIONS

✣ *Who or what has pushed you and caused you to grow and develop in new directions? How?*

✣ *What is your flat side? How can you be more well-rounded?*

28 DAVID M. NOER

David Noer, D.B.A., is an author, speaker, and executive coach. He has written six books and numerous academic and popular articles. His recently revised bestselling book, Healing the Wounds, *helps people and organizations recover from the trauma of layoffs. He is an Honorary Senior Fellow at The Center for Creative Leadership and Professor Emeritus of Business Leadership at Elon University.*

The Gain Is Worth the Pain

The great teachers of my life gave me a precious gift. It was not a tool, process, or technology; it was something deeper and more profound. They helped me understand that what really matters when helping people or organizations through change and transition is not technique but authenticity, vulnerability, and empathy. They taught me that connecting with others at the warm, messy, and unscientific level of the human spirit is a prerequisite for any methodology or process. I learned that technique without a grounding in empathy and vulnerability is sterile and artificial. I learned, as Larry Porter, one of my many great teachers, once said, "In the final analysis, the only tool worth a damn is our own warm body."

Larry's message has been reinforced and expanded by a number of other great teachers whose messages also reside in a unique and shadowy portion of my mind. Internalizing what they have been telling me has not been easy. I was, and at times continue to be, a resistant student. I grew up conditioned by dust bowl empiricism, where the operating theory was, "If you can't measure it, it doesn't exist." Unfortunately, this early tenet of the natural sciences has been adopted by many of the applied behavioral sciences, and it does not always support their effectiveness. My great teachers talk about concepts such as love, trust, vulnerability, empathy, and authenticity. "Try measuring those!" they shout in unison from their residence in my mind. "Empathy first, methodology second," they cry in rebuke whenever I become enamored of the latest gimmick or flavor of the month.

I've been lucky to have discovered many great teachers in my life. Collectively, they have helped block my tendency to escape from authenticity into technique. The magic part about my relationship with these teachers is that they are always there when I need them. There are many of them, and I don't always know who is on duty until she or he emerges. Some are well known, and others are not. In my experience, not all great teachers have fame or visibility, and not all well-known management gurus are great teachers. Some of the most famous are only a conduit for a single technique or methodology. They are solutions looking for problems.

My voyage of discovery began years ago when I was promoted to senior vice president of a large financial services holding company. Human resources was one of the functions that reported to me, and I found myself on what proved to be a "mission impossible." I wanted to drive out arbitrariness, hidden agendas, and power politics to make the organization more effective and people more creative and empowered. One of my great teachers emerged: Tony Tasca, who with his unique blend of humor and Sicilian worldliness introduced me to the basic values and processes of organization development. Through Tony, I was introduced to Pat Williams, who was just starting the Pepperdine MSOD program. As the founder and designer of the Pepperdine program, Pat has shaped the lives and perspectives of OD practitioners for more than twenty-five years. Pat and his late colleague Dave Peters taught me that the more in touch you are with what makes you tick and who you are, the more effective you will be in helping both people and systems change. I went to Pepperdine looking for a tool kit, and left with the dawning realization that I was the tool! I also discovered that as a tool I needed some calibrating and honing. You can only take someone as far as you've gone yourself.

My quest for external technique, however, still simmered and led me to the doctoral program at George Washington University. Maybe there I would find the right set of tools and methodologies. Instead I found Peter Vaill, another member of the growing cadre of great teachers whose messages live in that special corner of my mind. Peter, along with his colleague Jerry Harvey, taught me that knowledge and wisdom often take paths that resist measurement and control. I emerged from George Washington in midlife with a newly minted doctoral diploma and the increasing belief that dropping my defenses and establishing an authentic relationship with those I was attempting to help was of much more value than keeping control and applying objective tools and processes to management issues. It isn't that objective, external tools and techniques are bad or not useful; the point is that they are applied to human systems, and they require a context of authentic human interaction to work.

Life has a way of keeping us humble, and I was hit between the eyes with a large dose of humility in 1988. I had just left my well-paying corporate job and had accepted a lower salary for a more interesting faculty position at Duke University. Two weeks before I was to start, my wife, Diana, broke her neck in a car accident. Luckily she survived, albeit with some permanent damage, but not nearly as bad as what we anticipated at the time. I was thrust into a caretaker role and couldn't move to North Carolina and was therefore out of a job.

In this time of spiritual, emotional, and financial need, three great teachers emerged. All three gave me the same message: I knew more than I gave myself credit for, and if I stayed authentic and truly focused on the client's needs, as opposed to a methodology or technique, I too could be a great consultant and teacher.

The first lessons came from Dick Leider, who helped me get clear on my sense of purpose and bolstered my sagging ego and self-esteem by simply declaring me a "great spirit" and a "truth teller." He convinced me by providing the analytical part of me with concrete examples to support his declarations.

The next two lessons came from Dick Byrd and Marshall Goldsmith. They both brought me into consulting assignments with nothing to go on but trust (theirs, not mine) that I could do the work. "You know more than you know you know. Quit trying to analyze it and just do it!" said Dick as he thrust me into a complex and confusing client group.

Marshall phoned from California, expressed his concern over Diana's accident, and asked what I was going to do. "I think I'll try consulting, but I don't have any clients," I said.

"What are you doing next Tuesday?" asked Marshall. I didn't have any pressing engagements, so I joined him in Atlanta to work with one of his clients. That was it: no references, no letters of agreement, no conditions, no doubts (again from Marshall, not me). The kindness, faith, and unconditional optimism of both Dick and Marshall not only caused my declining self-esteem to soar, but also taught me the power of a positive self-fulfilling prophecy and reaffirmed that the currency of the realm in a helping relationship is applied human spirit, not method or technique.

As I look back on what I have accomplished and learned, I am grateful for the many teachers whose lessons live within me and deeply appreciative of their magical ability to materialize when I need them the most. They have helped me understand that help is in the perception of the person receiving the help, not of the person giving it. I have learned that technique and method are important but always need to be applied within the context of an authentic human relationship. My great teachers continue to help me understand that method, no matter how technical or complex, is easy. The hard part is dropping my defenses, being vulnerable, and establishing an authentic human connection.

QUESTIONS

✢ *If you are trying to lead, manage, or consult, have you gone through the necessary pain, struggle, and self-analysis that will allow you to drop your defenses, become vulnerable, and engage with your fellow humans (be they employees, bosses, or clients) in an authentic manner?*

✢ *Are you able to differentiate between the objective, predictable, and essentially nonhuman arena of techniques and methodologies and the subjective, warm arena of authentic human interaction, where transformation that can empower the soul and make the human spirit soar is possible?*

29 CHARLES E. DWYER

Charles Dwyer, Ph.D., has been on the faculty of the University of Pennsylvania since 1966. He is academic director for the Aresty Institute's Managing People Program in the Wharton School. He is also an associate professor in the Graduate School of Education. Dwyer has more than forty years of experience in educational, corporate, and organizational consulting. His client list includes IBM, Dupont, Xerox, MCI, Bell Atlantic, Westinghouse, R.J.R./ Nabisco, and others. His research and teaching cover a wide variety of topics, from interactive planning to group processes and personal development.

What Do You Do When Things Go Wrong?

Many years ago, I designed a program for the Wharton School called "The Effective Executive." It consisted of two weeks' worth of material and we gave it all over the country, usually in resort settings. We'd offer one core week and then several iterations for the second week. Anybody who took the first week was eligible to take the second week at a different location and a different time. In the early days of this program, I taught four of the ten days and recruited other people from the Wharton School to take on other topics.

Early in the program's history, one of the participants, to whom I am forever grateful, came to me and said, "This is not going well at all."

I was a little surprised by this, because I had screened the presenters for the program very carefully. They were often award-winning teachers in the university. He told me what he thought was going wrong with the material and my colleague's presentation.

It was a very difficult situation. On the one hand, I had some very unhappy participants; his report was not just of his own dissatisfaction. I discovered there were many people in the group who were dissatisfied with what was going on that morning. I came back in after the break with the faculty member who was making the presentation and said, "You know, we're going to have to hold it here. I understand there are some real issues; things aren't going well." And he said, "Well, I sensed that."

I asked him to step aside. I was the director of the program, and I had to take responsibility for what was (and what was not) going on. Even though my stomach was in my throat I stood in front of about forty people, all executives and high-level managers in corporate America. As comfortably and calmly as I could, I said, "I understand that things aren't going well. Can you give me some details?" The place erupted. I allowed them time to vent: the time they had given up, the money they had given up, this wasn't what they had expected, and so on.

I said, "Fine. Here are some alternatives for the rest of the week, and I want you to choose among the alternatives or tell me other things that you want me to try to do in the next few days." I broke them into small groups, had them discuss outcomes, and had a reporter and re-corder appointed to each group. When they came back together, they presented a series of suggestions to the planning group.

As stressful as this event was, it was a deep and valuable learning experience. It was emotionally difficult for me, not only as the primary presenter in the program, but also as the person ultimately responsible for the quality of the program and the satisfaction of the participants. On top of this was the fact that this was one of Wharton's offerings. There was a great deal in terms of image that had to be upheld. Word of mouth is often the most powerful way to get people to subsequent programs, and the program was being offered several more times that year. I could have easily panicked, but I didn't. Why, I don't know. I didn't get defensive, and I didn't rationalize the situation. I took it at face value and said I'm the one responsible, and these are the clients. Let's find out what they want and what's going wrong here and how we can fix it.

What was incredible was how positive things were from then on. This experience showed me that if you don't get defensive and don't rationalize, you are able to listen to people and they will be reasonable. You are then able to respond to their input. After that experience, I've commented to people on occasion that I've almost been tempted to make something go wrong within this kind of setting and then "make it right" for the goodwill that comes from the participants. I could imagine walking into the room calmly and saying, "Okay, folks, not everything always goes right in our lives."

The personal impact this experience had on me gave me a strong level of confidence when things go wrong. I now have a way of reacting to the unexpected; I know what that way is and I know that it works. Will it work in all situations? Probably not. However, there have been two or three situations, perhaps not as dramatic and intense as this example, in which my plans didn't go right, and I didn't swallow my stomach. I was calm because I knew what steps I was going to take and what the power of those steps was likely to be. And the difficult situation always turned around.

The other important outcome of this experience is that I don't worry about things going wrong. There's a certain level of concern in all of us when we're up in front of the room. You're a little bit like the pitcher in the ball game with everybody staring at you, and you either strike them out or you don't. I no longer feel that level of negative pressure to perform, because I know now that I can switch from pitching ideas to catching ideas when the plan needs to be changed.

QUESTIONS

✣ *What do you do when things go wrong?*

✣ *What checks can you put in place for yourself to gauge your effectiveness?*

Key Learning Points: Pain Is a Great Teacher

Why is it that the most painful experiences in our lives often lead to the most significant lessons? Each story in this section brought pain in some form to the writer. Yet each person was able to look past the pain and learn from the experience. What if he or she hadn't stopped to reflect? What would have been missed? R. L. Stine has a wonderful way of looking at the learning that is always inside the pain: "Sometimes when you least expect it, LIFE gives you a big ol' sock in the nose. Not to worry. With time, pain will pass, and from it you will have gained experience, which gives you information, which gives you objectivity, which gives you wisdom, which gives you truth, which gives you freedom from having to get a sock in the nose again."

After reading the preceding chapters, consider the following questions as you reflect on your own painful experiences:

‡ *Do you believe that pain presents opportunity? Why or why not?*

‡ *What are some ways in which you resolve a painful experience? What other experiences stimulate us to change? When do we move out of our status quo?*

‡ *Sometimes we learn the same lesson over and over. What is one lesson you seem to be stuck on?*

‡ *Sometimes people point to specific events in their lives and say, "If it weren't for [fill in the blank], I would not be where I am today." What key moments in your life could you point to in this way?*

MENTORS MATTER

RICHARD J. LEIDER
Does All That Make You Happy?

LOU TICE
Mentoring for Untapped Potential

CHIP R. BELL
Seven Lessons on Teaching and Training

ROBERT FRITZ
Pushing Through to the Next Level

JOEL BARKER
Lessons from My Coach

VIJAY GOVINDARAJAN
Contagious Influence Is a Wonderful Teacher

30

RICHARD J. LEIDER

Richard Leider is founder and chairman of The Inventure Group, a coaching firm devoted to helping individuals and leaders discover the power of purpose. As a pioneer in the coaching field, Leider has become an internationally respected author, speaker, and executive coach. He has authored eight books, including the international classic bestsellers Repacking Your Bags *and* The Power of Purpose. *For more than twenty-five years, he has led annual Inventure Expedition walking safaris in Tanzania, East Africa.*

Does All That Make You Happy?

An "inventure" expedition is an adventure within yourself. To inventure is to have the courage to look inside and discover your essence. Since 1983 I have led inventure expeditions to different places within the same regions in Africa. On one of my early inventures, we were backpacking in a corridor along the eastern edge of the Serengeti Plains. It was the first day of the trip, and our guide was a Masai chief by the name of Koyie. He and two of his warriors knew the area, and we were to camp with them at various villages along the way.

This was my first experience with Koyie and his first experience with anything like the people in our group. During our trek he carried nothing, and I carried a large, oversized pack containing a first-aid kit and lots of camping "necessities" as well as my own personal items.

Throughout the day's hike, I labored under the weight of my pack, and Koyie could see the effort I was expending under this burden.

We finally arrived at our destination. Tired, I threw my pack down on the ground and waited for the elder of the village to greet us and give us permission to stay there for the night. Koyie couldn't stand it any longer. He came over to me and very politely asked if I would show him what I was carrying. So I unloaded my pack and, object by object, shared the contents, including the bottles in my first-aid kit, Ziploc bags, Gortex, rain gear, and velcro—all the important things we take for granted that he had never seen before.

I had plenty of gear because we were going to be away from "civilization" for a while, and it took me a full ten minutes to unload the pack. Curious to see this spectacle, the entire village gathered around me to observe. Like Koyie, they had never seen anything like this before. Koyie, who had been watching patiently, looked at me, surrounded by enough products to stock a small dry goods store, and asked very simply but with great intensity, "Dick, does all this make you happy?"

I was stunned. There was something very powerful about Koyie's question. His words hit right at the heart of my deepest values. Immediately defensive, I said, "Well you know, I planned for this trip; I'm the leader," and I explained why I needed each item. Then I quickly stuffed everything back into my pack and went to my tent to collect myself. But I had been given a blinding glimpse of the obvious: I didn't need everything I was carrying. In a split second, Koyie's question had forced me to think about all I was carrying and why—not just on the trek but in my entire life.

I returned a short time later to the dozen or so people who made up the group and told them I was going to leave half of my things with the villagers. This prompted others in the group to start talking about what they were carrying. What is interesting, however, is that almost immediately the conversation shifted to our personal burdens and choices. What weights do we carry in our work lives and in our relationships? What journey are we on, and what do we need for that journey?

My load was much lighter after I'd reexamined my needs, and on the rest of the trip, I was happier for having repacked my bags. What Koyie helped me to do is what I now try to help other people do through both outdoor and indoor adventure. When people put down what they're carrying, look at what is inside, and determine the essentials, they are able to identify the essence of who they are. Once that essence is identified, the individual can pack accordingly for the journey ahead.

QUESTIONS

✢ *What's weighing you down?*

✢ *What would help you lighten your load?*

31 LOU TICE

Lou Tice is chairman and cofounder of the Pacific Institute, an educational corporation that operates on six continents and is based in Seattle, Washington. He is the author of Smart Talk for Achieving Your Potential; A Better World, A Better You; *and* Personal Coaching for Results, *with Joyce Quick; as well as the creator of the video bestseller* Investment in Excellence®. *Before founding the Pacific Institute with his wife, Diane, in 1971, Tice worked as a high school teacher and football coach. For nearly forty years, he has been in the business of helping people and organizations reach their potential.*

Mentoring for Untapped Potential

Most successful people have had at least one significant coach or mentor in their lives. What does a good mentor do that a role model doesn't? Think about it. Who have your mentors been? What did they do for you?

I'll bet they were people who could see more in you than you saw in yourself at the time. They saw you not only as you were, but also as you could be. They had a vision for you that was probably bigger than any you had for yourself. They weren't blind to your shortcomings and flaws, but they didn't focus on them. Instead, they helped you believe in your own strength, ability, and potential for growth. They inspired you and helped you to see possibilities for your life that you may not have seen otherwise.

Because your mentors had credibility in your eyes, you gave sanction to their visions. Then your self-talk followed suit: "Yes, that is possible for me. I could do that. I am like that." Your beliefs about yourself changed, and you began to act differently. Great coaches and mentors are so unshakably convinced that we have greatness in us, and their vision of what is possible for us is so clear and powerful, that they wind up convincing us, too.

MY FIRST MENTORS

I don't know where I'd be today if it had not been for the influence of people I looked up to who believed in me, especially those who were there for me when I was a kid. Sometimes I imagine the worst: I see myself as an aging, alcoholic football coach, mad at the world because I couldn't help anyone, even myself, to be a winner.

Then I think of Mr. Anderson, my sixth-grade teacher. He was a wonderful role model and mentor for me. He routinely put me in charge of the class at recess—a big responsibility—which made me feel like a capable leader. When he organized team sports, he sometimes put me in to play instead of more experienced, older players, even when those guys protested. I reasoned that I had to be worth it. Mr. Anderson had credibility in my eyes, and he made me believe I was someone special. So I made sure I behaved as if I was. I was determined that I wouldn't disappoint him or let him down. He went out of his way to set up experiences for me that reinforced my belief in myself, and I will always remember him for that.

I will also remember Evan Thomas. Evan was three years older than I, and we grew up in the same miserable neighborhood. Because of the heavy production demands of World War II, none of the kids where we lived had much adult supervision. Parents who were lucky enough to have jobs were putting in as many hours as possible, often working extra shifts. Older kids were pressed into service to care for younger ones. As a result, we often ran wild.

But Evan was different. He was physically, mentally, and morally strong. He was a Native American, but he didn't set himself apart from the rest of the kids. We thought of him as one of us but somehow better. You can imagine how it felt to have him notice me, to single me out, and to care enough about what happened to me to give me advice. When he told me to avoid certain people because they weren't good for me, I listened.

Evan was a fullback and a starter on the high school football team. I had always wanted to play football, too, but when I reached the ninth grade I was still small for my age, so I went unnoticed by the coach among the hundred or so boys who showed up for tryouts. I was sure I'd never make the team, but Evan wouldn't hear of it. "Here's what you need to do," he told me. "Don't let the coach out of your sight. You just go and stand by him every day, and tell him you want a uniform." I would never have dreamed of doing this on my own, but if Evan thought I was good enough to deserve a uniform, I figured it must be true. So I did what he suggested, and my persistence paid off. The coach gave me a uniform, and that's how I made the team.

The first time I went out with Diane, my wife, we double-dated with Evan and his girlfriend. I was going to take Diane on the bus, but that wasn't good enough for me, according to Evan. "You'll go with us in my car. I'll pick you up, and then we'll pick up Diane," he told me. "But what if this girl you're going out with doesn't want us along?" I asked him nervously, remembering that they were three years older. "Don't worry about that," Evan said. "If she doesn't like it, we'll just leave her home. You're my friend." Again, he made me feel important at a time when it mattered.

I heard that Evan died from a brain tumor a number of years ago. I was very disturbed by the news and especially disturbed that I had never told him how much his friendship and support had meant to me when we were kids. So I decided to talk to his mother. I drove across town to the old neighborhood and found the Thomas house.

Mrs. Thomas didn't remember me at all, but I told her what a fine person Evan had been. I explained how deeply he had influenced me and how important he had been to my growth, my character development, and my success in life. I told her that his attention and concern had meant the world to me at a time when I was in need of those things, and I told her how proud I had felt to have been Evan's friend. I told her I would never forget him, and I never will.

AFFIRM THE GREATNESS YOU SEE

The most powerful act any of us perform for others is to help them access their untapped potential, help them nurture and grow the best parts of themselves, those aspects that are hopeful, brave, persistent, inquisitive, hardworking, creative, resilient, kind, assertive, thoughtful, and resourceful.

What is our potential as human beings? No one knows, but we haven't even begun to approach our limits. Potential means capable of being, with a capacity for development. When we help others to value and believe in themselves, when we help them to feel supported in their choices no matter what the outcomes may be, we help them to grow into their greatness.

Saying that we shouldn't try to solve other people's problems or stand between them and the rightful consequences of their actions doesn't mean that we should do nothing. As mentors, we can offer much in the way of experience and wisdom. For instance, through skillful questioning, we can help people clarify the elements of a problem or decision they are thinking through. We can help them identify and evaluate their options and then create scenarios for various courses of action, imagining the outcomes of each. We can point out possibilities they may have missed and suggest alternatives. We can share our own strategies and the results of similar experiences that we have lived through, both successful and unsuccessful. (Sometimes our failures, mistakes, and aborted attempts can teach far more than those times of relatively smooth sailing.)

When we're sure we understand a situation, we can propose constructive actions or behavior changes—as long as we accept that our protegé is free to agree or disagree, to accept or reject our proposals, and as long as we don't disapprove or feel disappointed if our ideas are questioned or rejected. We can help others examine and adjust their self-talk, especially their affirmations and visualizations, and know themselves better. And we can help them review and evaluate the consequences of their decisions and what new decisions need to be made as a result of those consequences.

QUESTIONS

‡ *How can you be a better mentor to someone you live with or work with?*

‡ *What can you do to help another person reach his or her potential?*

‡ *What questions can you ask to help clarify the elements of a problem or decision someone else is working through?*

32
CHIP R. BELL

*Chip Bell is a senior partner with the Chip Bell Group
and manages the company's Dallas, Texas, office. An
internationally known speaker and consultant, he is the
author or coauthor of eighteen books, including* Managers
As Mentors, Take Their Breath Away, Magnetic Service, Instructing for Results, Understanding Training,
and Dance Lessons: Six Steps to Great Partnerships in
Business and Life.

Seven Lessons on Teaching and Training

"He was the best teacher I ever had." That was something I heard
often when I was growing up. The subject was my father; the fan club
was populated by his former high school students. By the time I reached
adulthood, I too had joined the "Ray Bell's a Great Teacher" fan club.

Ray Bell was never my teacher in the formal sense of the word.
By the time I arrived on the scene, he had left the teaching profession
to become a full-time banker and full-time farmer. But the teacher in
him never got turned off. Consequently, I was the lucky student of his
tutelage. His influence changed my life. His wisdom provided valuable
touchstones for my life's work as a trainer.

Here are the basic precepts of the Ray Bell approach to teacher
training.

1. *Great teachers are judgment free.* My father could be a stern taskmaster and a tough disciplinarian. He was very much a perfectionist when it came to performance. He expected the best, demanded the best, and demonstrated the best. However, when the goal was learning, he shifted to a completely different style. He suddenly became patient, even tolerant, and above all, nonjudgmental. When the objective was growth, he would treat the most inane question as a query reflecting insight just waiting to happen.

   He never snickered at my ignorance or scorned my naiveté. As a young man, I was much more likely to hear "Good try!" than to hear "Good gracious!" If I was busy working to acquire new skills or knowledge, leeway and latitude seemed to be his specialty. Great teachers are quick to confirm and slow to correct. They use body language that speaks acceptance and affirmation. They suspend critique, knowing judgment impedes risk taking and experimentation, both necessary for effective learning.

2. *Great teachers are participative partners.* "How 'bout going and getting the tractor and parking it in the barn?" Those sweet words were music to my ears when I was a ten-year-old growing up on a farm. It was Dad's way of nudging along my maturity. To get the very special privilege of starting, driving, and parking a large, expensive tractor was to feel trusted and respected. Dad's gesture made me feel thrilled and tall.

   The tractor-parking incident was more than a badge of being grown up. It was a symbol of partnership—I obviously relied on Dad, but at that moment, he trusted me enough to return that dependence. Great teachers perpetually seek ways to include and to partner. They would rather facilitate than lecture; they enjoy great questions more than smart answers. Dad joined in the pursuit, offering guidance, not expertise. He seemed to know that participation was the route to discovery and insight, an important building block for significant learning.

3. *Great teachers show perpetual curiosity.* My father asked me questions to which he did not know the answer. This trait always stood in stark contrast with what I witnessed in many of my friends' parents. My buddies frequently were asked questions with the slam of a spring-loaded bear trap. "Do you have any idea what time it is?" was not an "I lost my watch" kind of question. But Dad never used questions that way. When he asked a question, it always meant he was in search of an answer. I came to realize it was evidence of his perpetual curiosity.

   On family driving trips, we stopped at every historical road sign. We had long Sunday afternoon discussions provoked by queries such as, "What do you reckon Charles Dickens meant by that?" or "I wonder what Julius Caesar might have been feeling when that happened?" He took things apart just to see how they were made. He watched squirrels build a nest and then launched into a question-filled discussion of nest-building genes or weather-sensing skills. Great teachers never stop being curious. They view themselves as learners more than teachers. And they are both passionate and unabashed in their nonstop inquisitiveness.

4. *Great teachers find humor in most situations.* Dad was no comedian. In fact, he was a very shy man. But he enjoyed a great tease and was as quick to laugh at himself as he was to laugh with others. His humor was innocent and authentic, never contrived or sarcastic. Most important, he saw lightness in simple occurrences and enchantment in ordinary events. When he laughed, his expressions were bounteous and unbridled; his declarations of joy were always contagious.

   He intuitively knew that merriment was a key piece in the puzzle of learning. When learners encounter humor and joy in their teachers, they learn to laugh at themselves. The serious pursuit of growth must be coupled with an unserious process of growth. Ray Bell demonstrated that no matter how grave the destination, the trip needed to be a pleasurable one. He was the only teacher I had who could find a whimsical side to trigonometry or to Charles Dickens. The by-product of his example was my gaining an unerasable fondness for learning. That path has enabled me to become more and more a self-directed learner, learning simply for the joy of the trip.

5. *Great teachers show obvious pride.* Ray Bell experienced life firsthand. But he also experienced life secondhand. When my hard-earned competence was displayed in a public presentation, it was as if he too were on the stage, down the court, across the field, or in the pulpit. He was noticeably proud of the accomplishments of his children. And his pride never had a possessive "That's *my* boy," credit-seeking dimension. He simply seemed to be thrilled to see how it all worked out.

    Great teachers are proud to witness the effects of their teacher-learner relationships. They not only vicariously experience the growth of their learners, but they also look for ways to bear witness to the power of learning. Dad's sense of "Isn't that great!" or "Isn't that amazing!" was not an expression of surprise that I could actually do what he taught me. Rather, he was awed by the process of learning.

6. *Great teachers have impeccable ethics.* The most important lesson I learned from my father was that teaching is an ethical act. Effective teachers and trainers must be clean in their dealings with learners, not false, manipulative, or greedy. Good teachers are honest and congruent in their communications and actions. They never steal their learners' opportunities for struggle or moments of glory. They refrain from coveting their learners' talents or falsifying their own. Good teachers honor the learner just as they honor the process of mutual learning.

7. *Great teachers have great love for their students.* Ray Bell was all about love, and it infused his teaching relationship. When his former students spoke of their fond memories, it was clear they were speaking of someone they loved and of one who loved in return. Dr. Malcolm Knowles taught me that a good teacher or trainer must first and foremost love the learning. Ray Bell taught me an even deeper lesson: a great teacher or trainer must first and last love the learner.

QUESTIONS

✢ *If your learner were to give you a grade based on your own enthusiasm for learning, what grade would you get?*

✢ *In your learning or training programs, what would better equip participants to be more effective, lifelong learners?*

✢ *What role have you played in awakening the senses of your learners? What made them blush? What made them giggle?*

33 ROBERT FRITZ

For more than thirty years, Robert Fritz has been develop-
ing the field of structural dynamics through his work
related to the creative process as well as organizational,
business, and management issues. He is the founder of
Robert Fritz, Inc., Technologies for Creating®, Inc.,
and the Fritz Consulting Group. He is cofounder of
Choicepoint, Inc., producer of the management software
Structural Tension Pro™. Fritz is the author of five books,
The Path of Least Resistance, Creating, Corporate
Tides, The Inescapable Laws of Organizational Struc-
ture, *and* The Path of Least Resistance for Managers.
An active composer, Fritz has written film scores, operas,
symphonic music, and chamber music, and he was on the
faculties of the New England Conservatory of Music and
Berklee College.

Pushing Through to the Next Level

When people realize my background is in music, they ask me
how a conservatory-trained composer became interested in organizations and business. For me, learning to learn came directly from my
study of music. Their questions always make me think of one of my
music teachers, Mr. Poto.

A HARD LESSON

Attilio Poto was a member of the Boston Symphony Orchestra, a faculty member of the Boston Conservatory of Music, and a marvelous clarinetist. My first few lessons had to do with physical changes in my technique and my choice of curriculum. Mr. Poto decided that I would use a very difficult book of etudes, one I knew was well beyond my ability. I suggested an easier approach, but Mr. Poto said he had his reasons for the choice. So that was that.

The first week's etude was very difficult for me. I worked hard to perfect it, but I just couldn't play it very well. When it came time for my lesson, I tried to play the assigned etude, but I made many mistakes. Mr. Poto made suggestions and showed me how to play certain passages. I commented that I should spend another week practicing this piece, as I knew I needed more time and experience. As I was telling him this, Mr. Poto simply smiled at me and turned the page to the next exercise, one that was even more difficult than the one I had struggled with the previous week. I thought Mr. Poto wasn't a very good teacher.

The next week's lesson was terrible. Try as I might, I made even more mistakes, and my performance of the etude was dreadful. I was sure this time that Mr. Poto would give me another week to get it right. But instead he flashed his sweet smile and turned the page. "Don't you think another week . . . ?" He didn't. Poor man. He may have been a master clarinetist, but as a teacher . . .

Week after week was a repeat of the same pattern. I worked hard and couldn't play very well, but Mr. Poto just assigned me more difficult etudes. Finally, after six weeks of this torture, Mr. Poto taught me the real lesson. I began my usual complaint of "I can't learn this way," when Mr. Poto smiled and turned to the very first etude I had had such trouble with weeks before. "Play it, please," Mr. Poto instructed. I did. In fact, I played it well. The earlier difficulties had disappeared. Now I could do everything that had seemed impossible six weeks before. I played the piece much better than if I had spent the entire six weeks practicing that one etude.

Mr. Poto turned the page to the next etude. Again I could play it. It felt easy. With the third etude, it was the same story.

The lesson that Mr. Poto taught is still with me: The time to move ahead is before you think you are ready to move ahead. This is quite a revolutionary principle in light of our usual educational practices. Generally we believe that we must perfect something before we move to the next step. Moving ahead before you think you are ready is often uncomfortable. It feels wrong. It is counterintuitive. But all disciplines feel uncomfortable at first, because the physics of discipline involve doing something that is unnatural. It is natural to scratch when we have an itch. It takes discipline to not scratch.

It is not natural to learn how to ski, for example. The ski instructor says, "Lean down the mountain." But the new skier wants to lean away from, not toward, the bottom of the mountain. The way skis are designed, we are able to put on the brakes and control our speed only by leaning down. When we lean back, we "floor it," speeding up with less control than we would have otherwise, especially if we're beginners.

Discipline may not be natural, but it is the triumph of choice over instinct. With discipline, we are able to accomplish more than our instincts would ever allow. Therefore, make the choice to move ahead just before you think you are ready. That way you will assimilate the lessons you have been learning. Not only that, but you will create momentum that helps the learning process. Learning becomes easier and easier, even if what we are learning becomes harder and harder. This approach takes a high tolerance for being less than perfect at first.

THE SPIRIT

Another profound lesson I learned at the conservatory was also the result of an early experience with a teacher—this time one of my composition teachers. Early in the term he gave me an assignment. I quickly knocked it off and brought it to the next lesson. I gave it to him, and he began to study it. For several minutes the room was very quiet as he contemplated my work. Finally he said, "This is very good." I felt pleased and self-satisfied. Then he added, "But I know you're capable of more. And unless you are willing to reach for that, don't come back." I was shocked. But the feeling was more complex than simple shock. I felt found out, and I felt relieved that I was found out. Here was a teacher who wasn't fooled by my talent and natural ability. He was in the business of helping me reach my potential, not in the business of massaging my ego.

The level of commitment underlying my learning mode changed in that moment. "Do a good job" was replaced by "Reach for that which is highest in you." This was one of the best lessons I ever learned.

Learning in a vacuum rarely leads to the kind of profound discipline it takes to reach beyond ourselves into new worlds of ability and experience. Like building muscles, development doesn't happen all at once. It happens over time that is spent in the realm of the unfamiliar, disorienting, and perplexing. How high do we reach, what are our values, and what is the essence of our character? Discipline is the key, and aspiration is the spirit in learning that enables us to extend beyond our limits to reach our dreams.

QUESTIONS

✣ *How might you supply "music lessons" to others?*

✣ *Have you ever tried moving ahead before you have attained perfection?*

✣ *Can you reach a little more and try a little harder in your efforts?*

34 JOEL BARKER

Joel Barker is a noted futurist whose videos about paradigms have influenced the thinking of people worldwide about leadership. In 1975 Barker pioneered the application of paradigm shift theory to organizational vision. He also invented and refined tools that help reveal the long-term implications of change. Since the early 1980s, he has worked with most of the Fortune 500 companies and many other major institutions around the world. He is the author of Paradigms *and* Future Edge, *which was listed as one of the most influential business books of 1992 by* Library Journal. *Barker's company, Infinity Limited, Inc., is based in Minneapolis. His most recent video,* Innovation at the Verge, *can be found at* www.startharower.com.

Lessons from My Coach

Most of us count ourselves lucky when we have the chance to spend a year under the tutelage of a great teacher. I was lucky enough to spend five years with Evar Silvernagle, the finest high school swimming coach I could have asked for. My time with him began when I was on the swim team in the eighth grade. I was big and strong for my age and by midseason I had broken every school record for my age group.

One day as I was getting ready for practice, Coach Silvernagle walked in. He came over to me, introduced himself in a soft voice, and said, "I would like you to join the A squad, starting tomorrow." And then he left.

Me on the varsity team? I was overwhelmed. My teammates came over and congratulated me. What an honor! The next day I showed up for practice and Coach Silvernagle introduced me to his team. This team came from a long lineage of swimmers who over the past six years had not lost a swimming meet, including state championships, and had produced more than two dozen All-American swimmers. And this was in Rochester, Minnesota, a town with a population of less than 30,000. Coach Silvernagle concluded his introduction of me by saying, "We expect great things of Joel."

And so began my education by Coach Silvernagle. Now, let me give you the punch line first, so that there is no suspense. I never got any faster than I was in the eighth grade. I never earned a letter in the sport. But I stayed on the team for five years because of the greatness of Coach Silvernagle. He taught me lessons that I have used throughout my life. His leadership changed the way I related to the world. Here are the most important things I learned from him.

First, always be inclusive. Coach Silvernagle never cut anyone from his team. All the teams we competed against typically had twenty to thirty swimmers. I was never on a Silvernagle team smaller than sixty swimmers. The coach had a very simple philosophy: If you were willing to do the workouts, he always had a spot for you, no matter how slow you were. With that many kids in the pool, it should have been impossible to produce a good team, much less a state championship team. But he did, year after year.

Second, never stop experimenting. Coach Silvernagle was always trying to learn new ways to teach the strokes, new ways to execute dives, new ways to set up the workouts. He would start by saying that he had an idea, that he wasn't sure it would work, but would we be willing to try it? And then he would draw us into the experiment and ask us what we thought about it after we were done. And he always listened carefully to our answers. Whatever worked we applied with a vengeance.

Third, never give up on anyone. Remember that I never got any faster. Wouldn't you think he would have figured out that I had reached my peak and stopped trying to help me get better? Throughout the five years, every time I asked for help, he was there. He never complained; he always gave his time and attention. He acted as if there was always a chance something would change and you would become a great swimmer.

Fourth, excellence is the only target. Here was a man who understood continuous improvement and the purpose of excellence decades before it became a catch phrase in business. He never, and I mean never, talked down another team. Even when we knew we could shut out the other team, Coach spoke of the opponent with the greatest respect. When he described the match-ups of the various races, he invariably shared with us the other teams' best times, even if they had been achieved last season. Our times were always our most recent. He never talked about beating the other team, only about what our target goals were.

Once the captain of our team bragged to someone that we were going to "kill our opponent" that week. Coach Silvernagle heard about the boast, and the captain was not allowed to dress for the meet. No disrespect was allowed. There was a corollary to this rule: Never underestimate your opponents.

When Coach Silvernagle made up his swim list, it had two versions. Our best swimmers started the meet and swam until we had scored enough points to win the meet. The other team was always honored by having to compete against our strongest swimmers. But once we had the necessary points, Coach went to the second swim list. Our best sat down and the other swimmers got to compete.

What that meant, of course, was that many kids got to swim in the meets. It also meant that the swimmers from the other teams got a chance to take first and seconds. So, in his willingness to give his own swimmers a chance, Coach Silvernagle also allowed the other teams' swimmers to look good. He never ran up the score against weaker teams by continuing to use his strongest swimmers.

For five years I got to watch this man teach boys so much more than how to swim. I watched him teach how to win with honor and lose with dignity. I watched him give respect to the slowest and teach humility to the fastest. Many years later, another great teacher from Rochester gave his evaluation of Evar Silvernagle: "He was the most perfect man I ever met."

By the way, even though I was never more than a mediocre swimmer, I turned out to be a good swimming coach. Those years of instruction did pay off after all.

QUESTIONS

✢ *How might you be more inclusive with the members of your teams, your family?*

✢ *How might you experiment with routine procedures?*

✢ *Are you afraid to let all your team members get in the game?*

✢ *What would you really lose by giving everyone a chance to contribute to the team?*

35 VIJAY GOVINDARAJAN

Vijay Govindarajan is the Earl C. Daum 1924 Professor of International Business at the Tuck School of Business and founding director of Tuck's Center for Global Leadership. He is also the faculty codirector for Global Leadership 2020, Tuck's executive education program that focuses on global management and is taught on three continents. VG's has written numerous articles and has published six books, including The Quest for Global Dominance, *which was coauthored with Anil K. Gupta (Jossey-Bass, 2001). He is a popular keynote speaker and has been featured at such conferences as the* BusinessWeek *CEO Forum and The Economist Conference. In their new study, "The Emotionally Bonded Organization: Why Emotional Infrastructure Matters and How Leaders Can Build It," Govindarajan and coauthor Subroto Bagchi identify a critical new asset in Fortune 500 companies known as Emotional Infrastructure.*

Contagious Influence Is a Wonderful Teacher

Reflecting on the events that have affected and greatly influenced my life, I recall two experiences that prominently stand out. Although one of the experiences I would characterize as negative and the other positive, they equally shaped who I am as a person and how I practice my profession as a teacher. In relating these two events, I begin with the later, "negative" experience. Although this event occurred later on in my life, it is through this experience that I have been able to reflect, appreciate, and learn from the earlier experience.

Twenty years old, fresh out of college, I was one of twelve individuals recruited by one of the top five companies in India. I was invited to take part in a senior management-training program that had received thousands of applicants on a nationwide basis. My life was set. All I had to do was sit back and follow the track that laid out before me.

For more than three years, I participated in this high visibility program. I was exposed to the various operations of the organization ranging from marketing to manufacturing and finance. Toward the end of my third year, I began to realize that I hated what I was doing. The lack of freedom and flexibility was suffocating. I had to operate within a well-defined and structured box that tolerated little variation from the norm. When I first got this position, everybody, including myself, believed I had struck gold. The golden luster of organizational life was rapidly fading.

It became very clear to me that although this was considered to be one of the most progressive and well managed companies in India, only the top few leaders had any influence within the organization. It was a model in which the people at the top *Think,* and the people at the middle and bottom *Do.* I was not given a platform. I had a lot of good ideas, but there was no forum to be heard or ideas debated. The circle around me was sharply defined as to say, "You are not supposed to do a lot of thinking here." It struck me as depreciating the intelligence I had.

Concurrently, I observed people that were not much older than I, with Ph.D.s from American universities, would visit the organization and have an audience with the management teams. These people had written articles and shared their ideas from a large platform. They had influence upon the people with whom they shared their ideas. Seeing this and realizing that I had contributions and ideas that were being suppressed, I knew I had to find a better environment.

I resigned from my job despite the fact that my friends and family thought I was a bit crazy. I soon left India to pursue studies abroad in America.

The second experience spans a majority of my childhood and early adult years. I grew up in a small town called Ammamamalaimager. My father and grandfather moved there before I was born to pursue a more pious life. My grandfather is very religious, but more important, he is also very intelligent and widely read. Before he and my father came to Ammamamalaimager, my grandfather was a lawyer for the Maharajah.

Every Saturday and Sunday for as long as I can recall, my grandfather would leave our home early in the morning to teach and share ideas with an informal and ever-changing group of children. There was but one common denominator among these children: they were extremely poor and many were from what we call Untouchable Families (considered the "backward" classes of India). Under the banyan tree, in the center of town, my grandfather would spend hours helping these children with their schoolwork, exploring ideas, and more important, planting seeds of inspiration and aspiration.

When I was younger, I didn't understand why he was giving so much of himself. I found it an inconvenience more than anything else, because we couldn't eat lunch on weekends until he had returned. I didn't realize what he was doing until in my teens I saw some of these children come back to town as adults. They were now college professors and involved in other professions. They literally fell at the feet of my grandfather and thanked him for helping them.

My grandfather has influenced me a great deal in how I work with my students. I realized how exciting it is to participate in another person's goals. I find that my passion and excitement is contagious and, in fact, does influence others. I believe that aspirations provide a guide-wire for our goals. The higher the aspirations, the greater the goals and subsequent accomplishments.

Finally, from this experience, I have come to the realization that the most important and valuable aspect of teaching is respect for the student. When you have respect for someone, you really listen to what he or she has to say. As a teacher, you come from the point of view that the person has something to say and contribute, and as a result, you probe deeper as you question and explore ideas with the student. Through this approach everybody learns and as a teacher, you grow. In fact, the research idea that defined my career is the direct result of a classroom conversation.

Reflecting on these experiences, it is easy to see how my grandfather's values influenced my own. In many respects, he indirectly taught me a great deal. These shared beliefs were instrumental in giving me the confidence to leave the security and prestige of a top company to search and fulfill my own aspirations. In turn, one of my goals as a teacher is to alter the aspiration levels of my students.

There are three questions that I continually ask myself that you might ask yourself:

- Am I passionate about what I am teaching?

- Am I learning? Am I becoming different? Am I growing intellectually?

- Am I altering the aspirations of my students? Am I helping them to set their sights higher than they previously envisioned?

Key Learning Points: Mentors Matter

People constantly influence our lives. They reach, direct, support, and nurture us. The mentors or helpers in these stories ranged from traditional teachers to unlikely sources of influence. Clearly, individuals can be mentors without knowing that they are playing this role. The power of our mentors may not lie in a particular model they give us, but may be in their capacity to wake us up to an important lesson, the significance of which we realize only later. And we are often unaware of the mentoring that could be ours simply for the asking! All around us are opportunities to mentor others and receive gifts from those who fill our lives. Think about your willingness and capacity to mentor others, as well as your openness to having others mentor you.

After reading the preceding chapters, consider the following questions in your exploration:

✤ *How have mentors contributed to your learning?*

✤ *Who have your mentors been?*

✤ *How did you find your mentor, or how did your mentor find you?*

✤ *How have you contributed to someone else's learning?*

✤ *In what ways could you mentor others around you?*

✤ *What did you learn from being a mentor?*

✤ *Who was your most effective mentor? Why?*

✤ *What behaviors and attitudes are necessary for a learner to get the most out of a mentor?*

Afterword

JODI KNOX

Dr. Jodi Knox is the Founding Director of Action Dialogue Associates, a leading firm specializing in executive coaching and facilitating dialogue processes that lead to shared understanding, committed action, and results. Jodi has extensive experience in strategic leadership development specializing in behaviorally-focused executive coaching and peer coaching for leaders. Bringing significant industry experience to her work, Jodi creates new communications and dialogue approaches for action and develops talent strategies and tactics to meet business required talent demands. She has consulted with many Fortune 50 companies on leadership development programs and conducted practical research to evaluate ROI and leverage the outcomes. She can be reached at jknox@actiondialogue.com or (888) 237-5634.

Forums for Learning

We hope that you will use the stories in this book to create experiences that stand on their own, to inspire new interactions with partners and groups, or simply to enhance your own self-development. This section offers experiential approaches that may be used to drive leadership learning and may be tailored to meet specific learning needs. Whether you are flying solo, in a paired relationship, or establishing a group forum for learning, the following three approaches offer suggestions to spin your thinking and take your learning to the next level, personally and professionally.

We learn much about our own thinking and framing of problems by looking at how the authors of these stories approached situations. While the reflective questions will help you gain additional insight into yourself, even greater freedom and opportunity comes from anticipating your development needs and seeking experiences, resources, and help to support real-time learning initiatives.

1) LEARNING ON YOUR OWN

Is there a leadership attitude, key learning, or way of framing situations from this rich compendium of stories that hit you head-on, where you said, "I need to adopt this way of thinking, or acting, and let go of my old way?" These opportunities for informal learning can be designed by you and for you. Here are a few steps to try:

- Take just one of those compelling attitudes, or key learnings, and commit to applying it to an upcoming situation, or set of experiences. Consciously focus on practicing the principle or new attitude in your affairs. These stories have the power to spark planned learning and growth in the challenges and experiences that surround us.

- Be deliberate. Expect growth to feel uncomfortable. Walk through the discomfort found in doing it differently. For the discomfort *is* the change itself—the learning and growth that *is* happening in practicing a new way of acting or thinking. When flying solo, remember you cannot think yourself into a new way of acting—you must act yourself into a new way of thinking.

- Use these stories with clear intention. Apply the attitude or frame they shared to your experiences. Then share your results, experiences, stories, and insights with others.

- Ask others for their feedback on what you experienced. What suggestions might they have for you in practicing the self-learning principle you identified and applied?

- Recruit others as needed to keep you going. Others can help you remain focused and help you reflect on your unique experiences. Practice; repetition is important.

Once you feel you have mastered a new attitude, or integrated a new learning, move on! Pick another key learning or a different theme that would serve you in your personal success plan. Continue this intentional, planned learning path and experience the freedom in developing both personally and professionally.

2) LEADERSHIP LEARNING IN PAIRS

At times it is easy to take for granted what we have accomplished during our lives. The stories each of us has to share are powerful learning resources, valuable not only to ourselves but to the people around us. Each of us has experiences that have provided incredible learning. And, it is important not only to remind ourselves of the experiences that have brought us to where we are, but also to share our stories with others so they can gain greater insight into who we are.

The next level of commitment and potency in consciously driven learning approaches is learning in pairs, or dyads. This is an incredibly effective vehicle to drive your personal or professional learning. Having a peer, or buddy, in your development approach delivers even greater impact and accountability. And, it's more fun! A partner can help you execute your learning goals and action plans while you do the same for them. Here is an effective approach to try:

- Find the right learning partner by considering the following two frames: Is there a peer, or partner, in your professional life who shares the desire to develop in a similar area? Or, is there a peer whom you see as already possessing the mind-set you want or who acts in a way you would like to master?

- Identify your partner from one of those two frames and make an agreement to support each other in your leadership learning efforts.

- Frequently check in with each other to support purposeful decision making and fast-forward actions. This is a great way to build strong professional relationships while also creating rigor and acceleration around your learning commitment.

Using paired relationships where another person has your best interests at heart, and reciprocally you have theirs, accelerates learning and keeps the emphasis on your personal development while you practice, gain insight, and build skills for your future.

3) CREATING LEADERSHIP LEARNING IN GROUPS

As you may have experienced in reading this collection, stories focus attention on what is important and why. This attention creates a powerful cascading effect in a group. With the focus on intentional learning and development, groups of four to six individuals can coach one another on a learning topic or issue of their choosing. In this way, group forums give clients the opportunity to drive experiential leadership learning and personal development deeper into the organization, on a larger scale, in a cost effective manner. Here's how it can be done:

- Rotate the group's focus from one person to the next with each group session. Or, alternatively, focus on multiple participants receiving coaching from the group per session on the experiential learning topic identified.

- Think purposefully about upcoming situations; what message do you want to send to your organization or what learning do you want to derive from your experiences? Practice demonstrating that learning principle through your actions, attitudes, and conversations.

- Utilize a personal board of advisors, a trusted group of colleagues, to collectively develop one another in a unique blend of topics based on individual needs. Solicit their input and feedback on actions taken and course corrections as needed.

- Take the impact of these stories seriously. Record stories as your group develops their shared experiences and consequently their own repertoire of learning journeys. Use these stories consciously to communicate a vision, provide direction, display humanness, and strengthen the culture of your teams and organizations.

- Be present to the real-life learning opportunities in front of you. Practice the personal learning plan you have chartered. Capture the learning and develop the messages and personal stories that you wish to communicate. Through the group's mentoring, stories provide powerful mechanisms for conveying the values and beliefs that illuminate one's own personal leadership identity and the organizational culture desired. Meet as a group to reciprocally support one another and sharpen the learning and skills around each goal.

This group approach to learning and storytelling can galvanize a community, reinforce desired behaviors, and accelerate intentional leadership learning in your organization. Tell others the stories surrounding your experiences, the lessons learned, that are supportive of the culture you want to nurture. Spark their thinking in the direction of their own learning experiences. After all, what we pay attention to and practice grows. Learn like a leader and share your learning journeys to make a difference.

The rich stories from this collection can serve as a basis for mapping a personal leadership-learning plan. Greater perspective and ways of acting are gained by practicing alternative routes to confronting difficult situations. We hope the learning forums outlined here begin to bridge the gap between identifying a desired leadership-learning need and cultivating new approaches and skills where the most important development occurs—in the job experience.

Epilogue

RICHARD STONE

Richard Stone has developed several successful programs for teaching patients, their families, and medical professionals how to bring the practical applications of storytelling into their therapeutic work. Under the auspices of the StoryWork Institute, which he founded in 1993, Richard developed training programs for team building, leadership development, and diversity for a variety of healthcare institutions, as well as assisted organizations such as the Red Cross and the YMCA to more clearly articulate their stories to enhance fundraising effectiveness. He has been a key member of the IDEAS Innovation team since 2003, and is now their StoryAnalytics Master. He is the author of The Healing Art of Storytelling, Stories: The Family Legacy, *and* The Kingdom of Now, *and he created the award-winning board game,* Pitch-A-Story. *He has also authored several collections of stories for healthcare clients as diverse as hospitals and pediatric practices. In addition, he has written a number of entertainment products, including* On the Spot, *a feature romantic comedy, and* Sprinkles, *a sitcom.*

The Power of Stories

Many things are so intimate to the human experience that we rarely think about them, such as the wisdom we receive from listening to stories and our ability to laugh at ourselves—two traits that distinguish us from animals. Consider laughter for a moment. While seated with some friends one evening, one individual shared that he had recently taken his nine-year-old son on a meditation retreat. The conversation wandered to how children seem to think they know everything, which prompted me to comment that now that his son had sat at the feet of a guru, he might have gone from being a "smart ass" to a "wise ass." Everyone chuckled. But when I asked the group to reflect on why they had laughed, no one could give a reasonable explanation. I can only wonder at what is encoded in our shared human experience that makes some things funny and others dry and humorless. It is difficult to explain, but undeniable.

The powerful role that stories play in our lives also seems indisputable, but just as mysterious as laughter. They can move us to tears, teach us profound lessons, open up unforeseen ways to understand our lives, and transform our pain into something wondrous. But why? Consider for a moment what it is about the following story that, I hope, leaves you with a smile and a nod of recognition about its inherent truth.

A young man once went to a guru and asked him how he might obtain wisdom. After some thought, the guru responded, "To gain wisdom, my son, you must have good judgment." This response gave the young student something to ponder, but he wasn't wholly satisfied. A few days later he returned to the master and inquired what it would take to attain good judgment, if that was indeed the path to wisdom. Once again, the guru pondered the question, then smiled, saying, "To develop good judgment, you must have a great deal of experience." For a while this answer mollified the young man's curiosity, but seeds of discontent began to sprout. If he needed experience to acquire good judgment, and good judgment to gain wisdom, how could he get the appropriate experience? Once again he approached the teacher. Without hesitation, the wise man responded, "Oh, that is simple. To get experience, you must exercise a great deal of bad judgment!"

In such a simple fashion, stories can convey much that other forms of communication cannot. Some of the world's greatest philosophers have devoted tomes to the subject of wisdom, but I have never heard a more elegant definition than the one in this story. Nor are these philosophers' explanations as accessible to the common intellect. Perhaps this is why we have begun to re-embrace stories at a time when so much of our information sharing is compressed into sound bites and we are bombarded daily by a perplexing glut of data. Stories are an antidote to both, feeding something in us that is hungry for more than bare-bones facts and distilled information, while also making complex ideas understandable and even actionable. Because of a story, people can make remarkable changes in their behavior and overall lives. Large groups have changed the course of history through the unadorned sharing of uncomplicated faith stories. There is something profound and mysterious here, but as natural as breathing.

Stories also give us so much more than a mere lesson. They provide a context, and when we hear a good one, like laughter, they are unmistakable in their impact on our being. In some work I did recently for a major Fortune 500 company around the area of knowledge management, I discovered that the company has devoted much time and money to capturing the lessons it has learned from past projects. Somewhere along the way, top management had concluded that this activity would be important to the long-term vitality of the organization. When completed, the documents pertaining to this project are neatly stored in a library in the company's corporate headquarters. You would think that a place that contains the collective wisdom of the company would be a hotbed of activity and learning, but the opposite is the case. Not one soul has ever gone there! The reason should be apparent: When the lessons of the past are offered without the stories that led to them, it is difficult, if not impossible, for us to learn from the experience of others. If the lessons were all that mattered, then it would be simple to raise children, for example. We'd just give them the manual containing the distilled wisdom gained from the follies of our own youth, and they would adjust their behavior accordingly. The absurdity of such a proposition is evident. But that is in fact what happens in business every day, with equally ineffective results. It also shows up in career development and management books.

By contrast, the stories contained in this volume are so powerful that they inspire us to learn in a way that nothing else can—giving us something precious that we could expect to receive only from a grandparent with whom we have had a long and intimate relationship. When we hear a story, we get to travel vicariously down the same path as the person who first learned from an experience. If the authors in this book had simply told us what they had learned without sharing how they came to these insights, the lessons would be flat, uninteresting, and probably devoid of value. By wrapping the conclusions in the cloak of a story, the lessons become digestible, nourishing our soul as well as our intellect.

As a way to learn, perhaps none understood the technology of stories better than Native Americans. My best teacher in this regard has been Paula Underwood, a descendant of the Oneida people. From an early age, children in her tradition would be taught using this age-old communication tool. Unlike our tradition of fables, in which we tell the story and then tell the reader or listener what the story means, when elders in this learning way concluded the telling of a story, they would gently ask a child to reflect on its meaning. The Oneida understood thousands of years ago that as we listen to or read a story, it is strictly a right-brain affair. It is felt, sensed, and translated into images in our mind. While there may be some learning at this point, it is incomplete. Only when we are asked, "What might you learn from this story?" do we move over to linear thinking in the left brain, teasing out the many lessons that the story holds for us. Marrying these two modes of knowing is what leads to whole learning. Using this simple approach, it is amazing what can be revealed by a mere story. There may be lessons that even the teller failed to see or expect. On the other hand, if we are told what the story means, we are robbed of the opportunity to make these important connections for ourselves, and learning is short-circuited. If you ask this learning question at the conclusion of each story in this volume, you may be surprised by the profound insights and thinking that emerge unaided by the wisdom of the teller.

Stories also refer us to the rich texture of our own experience. In that way, they are soulful. As we hear a story, we find ourselves drawn into our imagination, making subtle associations with past events in our own lives. Stories, like waves from the ocean, wash over us, bringing to the shores of our consciousness rich material from the water's depths, while also washing away sand from the shore to expose layers beneath the surface. You can't hear a story without being delivered to the currents of your own experience, with many related stories being stirred up and emerging into full view.

I also have found it useful to liken learning stories to windows that at times reveal the intricate interior of the experience of people who have traveled difficult roads, and at other times reflect back to us an image of ourselves. When we frame our own experiences in the light of the experiences of others, the reflection often exposes a facet of our own person that was previously obscured or unclear. While houses are similar in many respects, each home is remarkably unique. Likewise, looking into a house through different windows offers different perspectives on the same room. As we proceed with decorating our own interiors with rich textures and furnishings that enhance our lives, it is often useful to see how others have approached the same task. Surely our tastes will differ, and we would never do things exactly the way another would.

But you can't help but get ideas of how you might add a little color here, or combine the things you already have in a new and unusual way that is both pleasing to the soul and elegant to the eye. In building our own lives we can't help but benefit from seeing how others have approached the assignment, and learn from their mistakes and their triumphs.

I recently heard Syd Lieberman, a wonderful storyteller, share his definition of humor: "Things are funny when we work our life from the opposite side of the street." Think about it. When we are in the middle of the trials that life so readily dishes up, we rarely have any perspective, and certainly there is nothing funny about our pain or the difficulties we endure. But if we go across the street and watch the unfolding drama through the perspective of time, things often take on a certain absurdity, leading us to laugh and even learn. Why? Perhaps it is because when we see our lives through the prism of a story, it may be the nearest we can come to the jocular viewpoint of the laughing Buddha. That's what I think this lovely volume of stories does for us. It allows us to see with clarity our lives reflected back through the lens of others' experiences. I hope these tales will enrich you as they have filled me with their humanity and wisdom. And, if we take a few steps back, ever mindful of the open manhole as we cross the street, perhaps we will learn the most important lesson of all—to find understanding, and even humor, in the seemingly senseless events, failures, and painful losses that weave their way through our lives.